D1432500

BRAND LOYALTY
MEASUREMENT AND MANAGEMENT

SERIES ON MARKETING MANAGEMENT

Series Editor: **FREDERICK E. WEBSTER, Jr.**
The Amos Tuck School
of Business Administration
Dartmouth College

GEORGE S. DOMINGUEZ, *Marketing in a Regulated Environment*
ROBERT D. ROSS, *The Management of Public Relations: Analysis and Planning External Relations*
VICTOR WADEMAN, *Risk-Free Advertising: How to Come Close to It*
FRANK H. MOSSMAN, W. J. E. CRISSY, and PAUL M. FISCHER, *Financial Dimensions of Marketing Management*
JACOB JACOBY and ROBERT W. CHESTNUT, *Brand Loyalty: Measurement and Management*

Brand Loyalty Measurement and Management

JACOB JACOBY
Purdue University

ROBERT W. CHESTNUT
Columbia University

A RONALD PRESS PUBLICATION

JOHN WILEY & SONS, New York • Chichester • Brisbane • Toronto

Library of Congress Cataloging in Publication Data

Jacoby, Jacob.
  Brand loyalty.

  (Wiley series on marketing management)
  "A Ronald Press publication."
  Bibliography: p.
  Includes index.
  1. Brand choice. I. Chestnut, Robert W., joint author. II. Title.

HF5415.3.J32   658.8'34   77-28660
ISBN 0-471-02845-2

Printed in the United States of America

10 9 8 7 6 5 4 3 2 1

Dedicated to our parents
David and Frances,
Miller and Mildred

Series Editor's Foreword

Marketing management is among the most dynamic of the business functions. On the one hand it reflects the everchanging marketplace and the constant evolution of customer preferences and buying habits, and of competition. On the other hand, it grows continually in sophistication and complexity as developments in management science are applied to the work of the marketing manager. If he or she is to be a true management professional, the marketing person must stay informed about these developments.

The Wiley Series of Marketing Management has been developed to serve this need. The books in the series have been written for managers. They combine a concern for management application with an appreciation for the relevance of developments in such areas of management science as behavioral science, financial analysis, and mathematical modeling, as well as the insights gained from analyzing successful experience in the marketplace. The Wiley Series on Marketing Management is thus intended to communicate the state-of-the-art in marketing to managers.

Virtually all areas of marketing management will be explored in the series. Books now available or being planned cover advertising management, industrial marketing research, brand loyalty, sales management, product policy and planning, public relations, overall marketing strategy, and financial aspects of marketing management. It is hoped that the series will have some effect in raising the standards of applied marketing management.

FREDERICK E. WEBSTER, JR.

Hanover, New Hampshire
June 1977

Preface

This book is foremost a practical one. Written to be of immediate value to the marketing manager, it deals with an issue logically prior to the application of any theory or model of brand choice behavior. That issue is measurement. Quite simply, how do we attach numbers in some meaningful way to one very important aspect of consumer behavior, namely, brand loyalty?

For more than five decades marketing practitioners and consumer theorists have talked of the "loyal" consumer. Although originally confined to the context of brands and later extended to include stores, the concept of buyer loyalty has spread to include such topics as industrial purchasing, service agreements, bank accounts, and even medical prescriptions. Given that "brand choice can be viewed as encompassing most of the field of consumer behavior" (Wind, 1975), it is understandable that loyalty has become one of the most frequently studied aspects of the purchasing process. It has done so, however, with minimal serious consideration to the issue of measurement. As of now, there is no general agreement about what constitutes an appropriate conceptual or operational definition of loyalty

This lack of agreement has produced confusion regarding loyalty—confusion reflected in both the marketing literature and in managerial decision-making. How,
for example, is the manager to identify the loyal consumer when the same person is defined as loyal by one
criterion but considered nonloyal by another? What
really constitutes loyalty? Will it add substantially to the
understanding of why a buyer stays with or switches
from a given brand? Ultimately, with knowledge of the
appropriate changes in promotional advertising, or image, is it possible to manage loyalty's presence in the
market more effectively?

Answers to these and related questions will be forthcoming only after the measurement issue has been satisfactorily resolved. Before we can hope to understand and
influence brand loyalty (and its impact on sales), we must
have a clear idea of what we are attempting to measure
and what operations are appropriate for measuring it.

Chapter 1 begins to provide an answer to the first of
these questions. It differentiates brand loyalty (BL) from
the overlapping and more general phenomenon of repeat
purchase behavior (RPB). It does so through contrasting
stochastic theories of brand choice with a deterministic
approach to BL. Neither of these research philosophies
is entirely rejected. Although our orientation primarily
reflects a deterministic view, both philosophies are
considered to be useful tools in the development and
evaluation of marketing strategies.

Chapters 2 and 3 consider BL in terms of the approaches that have been taken to measure it. Specifically, Chapter 2 traces the historical development of
these definitions, while Chapter 3 provides an organized
compilation of the more than 50 different ways of
measuring BL now available. Information on each measure's sensitivity, reliability, and validity is also
presented.

It quickly becomes obvious that just describing these
measures is not enough. There is a need for agreement on
one or a select few clear conceptual definitions to which

the various operational measures can be related. Chapter 4 develops the necessity for and rationale underlying conceptual definitions in general and goes on to provide a specific conceptual definition of BL. Although composed of six necessary and sufficient components, the essence of this definition resides in its emphasis on underlying psychological evaluative processes.

The concluding chapter, Chapter 5, describes the practical value to be derived by marketing managers from having a valid definition and measures of BL.

Thus the primary objective of this volume is to provide the marketing manager with an understanding of what BL is and is not and how it can be measured and used. A secondary objective is to stimulate the academic thought and research needed to bring BL measurement to a higher plateau of sophistication and utility.

The senior author acknowledges with warm appreciation the fact that portions of his early (circa 1968–1972) thinking in regard to BL were influenced by interactions with his graduate students at the time, especially with Jerry C. Olson. Also appreciated is the giant United States manufacturing concern that sponsored an early, briefer proprietary version of this monograph but whose policy it is to remain anonymous in instances such as these. Finally, we both extend our thanks to Maureen Tate, typist extraordinaire, for her patience, expertise, and attention to detail through numerous revisions of this manuscript.

JACOB JACOBY
ROBERT W. CHESTNUT

West Lafayette, Indiana
New York, New York
March 1978

Contents

ONE

The Significance of Brand Loyalty for Marketing Management, 1

Stochastic versus Deterministic Views of Repeat Purchase, 2
The Managerial Implications of Brand Loyalty, 5

TWO

Trends in Brand Loyalty Measurement: A Historical Perspective, 7

Brand Loyalty Measures: 1923–1976, 10
Synthesis and Trends, 28

THREE

A Comprehensive Review of the Operational Definitions of Brand Loyalty, 33

Behavioral Indices of Brand Loyalty, 35
Evaluation of the Behavioral Indices, 41
Attitudinal Indices of Brand Loyalty, 47
Evaluation of Attitudinal Indices, 50

Composite Indices of Brand Loyalty, 52
Evaluation of the Composite Indices, 56
Chaos in Researchland: The Sorry Status of Brand Loyalty
 Measurement, 57

FOUR

**A Manager's Guide to Conceptual Definitions, Theory, and
Construct Validation, 67**

Conceptual and Operational Definitions, 68
Problems with Purely Operational Definitions, 71
The Necessity for Conceptual Definitions, 75
A Conceptual Definition of Brand Loyalty, 80
The Place of Conceptual Definitions in Formal Theory, 85
Construct Validation: Ensuring That Our Measures Reflect Our
Concepts, 90

FIVE

**Areas for Marketing Application Involving Brand Loyalty
Measurement, 101**

Market Share, Market Segments, and Brand Loyalty, 102
A Theoretical Perspective on the Development of Brand
Loyalty, 105
Areas of Marketing Applications, 115
Conclusion, 119

References, 121

Supplemental References, 133

Author Index, 151

Subject Index, 155

BRAND LOYALTY
MEASUREMENT AND MANAGEMENT

ONE

THE SIGNIFICANCE OF

Brand Loyalty

FOR

Marketing Management

We begin with two assumptions. First, most consumer product firms are interested in selling more of their product(s) and doing so with the greatest possible efficiency. Second, particularly with established firms marketing inexpensive and frequently purchased consumer products (i.e., nondurables), it is *not* the single sale that is of consequence; rather it is repeated sales to what it is hoped is an ever-expanding group of customers that is the objective. In other words the long-term success of a particular brand is based, not on the number of consumers who purchase it only once, but on the number who become repeat purchasers.

It stands to reason, then, that management will have at least the following four basic objectives:

1. To change the occasional purchaser of its own brand into a repeat purchaser.
2. If reasonable, to increase the amount consumed by the repeat purchasers of its own brand.
3. To attract purchasers from competing brands (and thereby inhibit repeat purchases of these brands).
4. To maintain high levels of repeat purchase for its own brand by "inoculating" repeat purchasers against brand switching.

These four objectives all reflect different aspects of one basic goal, namely, to increase market share. As C. Davis Fogg, Manager of Market Planning for the Electronic Products Division of the Corning Glass Works, noted: "Gaining and keeping significant market share is considered by many to be the single most important key to high, long-term profitability and substantial profit volume" (1974, p. 38). All forms of repeat purchase behavior (RPB)—including what we shall call brand loyalty (BL)—are inextricably related to developing, maintaining, and protecting market share.

STOCHASTIC VERSUS DETERMINISTIC VIEWS OF REPEAT PURCHASE

How, then, is the manager to understand the phenomenon of repeat purchase so as to achieve the aforementioned objectives and thereby increase control over market share? The marketing literature has adopted two quite different philosophies in approaching this question. To set the stage for much of what is to follow, let us consider these in some detail.

The first philosophy is represented by a number of mathematical models known as the "stochastic theories" of buyer behavior. At their core is the suggestion of a strong random (i.e., purely chance) component underlying basic changes in the market structure (cf. Bass, 1974; Ehrenberg, 1972; Herniter, 1973). Although it does not seem reasonable to maintain that individual consumers are going through life flipping coins (at least one would hope that this is not the case, especially for industrial buying), the stochastic argument is quite powerful when applied to buyer behavior in the aggregate. As Bass (1974, p. 2) asserts: "even if behavior is caused but the bulk of the explanation lies in a multitude of variables which occur with unpredictable frequency, then, in practice, the process is stochastic."

Repeat purchase behavior (i.e., some degree of repetitive purchase of the same brand by the same buyer) appears to be one such behavior. Consider the following correlations obtained in investigations of RPB:

- The larger the building lived in, the greater the likelihood of RPB (Frank, Douglas, and Polli, 1968).
- Working wives are more likely to engage in RPB (Anderson, 1972).
- High sociability with neighbors is related to a greater likelihood of RPB (Carman, 1970).

The list could continue at some length. Behind each correlation would seem to lurk a new explanation for RPB. The building size relationship, for example, was most likely an artifact of distribution. That is, "large building dwellers" in this study lived in downtown Chicago, where small retail outlets forced the consumer to choose from a restricted set of brands. Working wives were seen to "economize" actively on their time and hence considered fewer brands, often resorting to a favorite or easy choice, in purchasing. High sociability implied greater word-of-mouth communication, and thus, one might attribute RPB to the lack of any personal involvement in brand choice and to the suggestions of friends. And so our list might continue until the overall picture of causation looked very much like the situation described by Bass: one of numerous variables affecting RPB with unpredictable frequency (i.e., a stochastic process).

The implications of this reasoning for the marketing manager are twofold. On the positive side the assumption of a stochastic process greatly facilitates his ability to model and thereby predict gross fluctuations in the amount of RPB. From Lipstein's (1959) introduction of Markov Chains to the more recent developments by Bass and his associates (cf. Bass, Jeuland, and Wright, 1976; Bass and Wright, 1976), probabilistic models of buyer behavior and brand switching have proved valuable in the design and evaluation of marketing strategies. On the negative side, however, a major drawback pervades the very nature of this stochastic philosophy. By its acceptance the marketing manager abdicates or, at the very least, assumes severe limits on his ability to exert any influence over RPB. If what we observe in terms of buyer behavior is so complex as to present a random phenomenon, then the managerial objectives mentioned earlier must be viewed as being outside the reach of any advertising or marketing activity.

Is this really the case? Must we conclude that the marketing manager is unable to influence the presence of RPB? The second research philosophy provides a rather emphatic "no" in response. Best labeled "determinism," this approach assumes the existence of one or, more likely, some limited number of cause(s). Repeated purchase of the same brand by the same consumer does not just happen; rather, it is the direct consequence of something underlying the consumer's behavior. By isolating and arriving at an understanding of such underlying causes, the marketing manager should be able to alter the very existence of RPB. The deterministic philosophy embraces the possibility of attaining the aforementioned management objectives by taking consistent brand-purchasing behavior out of the realm of chance.

Unfortunately, determinism has met with little generalizable success in its attempts to fully explain RPB. The very same reason, that stochastic models have proved so useful, accounts for determinism's lack of success, for RPB is multicaused. From small children demanding that their mother purchase a specific brand to the effect of end-counter displays or shelf space, RPB is the net result of many influences. Although it serves an academic interest for deterministic-oriented investigators to continue isolating cause after potential cause, it is of little practical use to the marketing manager. The plain fact of the matter is that he cannot hope to monitor and control so many diverse factors. What, then, is the future of determinism as related to the phenomenon of RPB?

The answer lies in a more realistic acceptance of the limits of this philosophy. On the assumption that determinism cannot explain the totality of RPB in a way that is of real value to the marketing manager, it behooves adherents of this philosophy to narrow their focus and address something within the general limits of its ability. As advanced elsewhere (Jacoby, 1971a, 1971b; Jacoby and Kyner, 1973; Jacoby and Olson, 1970) and described more fully in Chapter 4, our position is that a deterministic orientation can be meaningfully applied to a distinct subset of RPB, a subset we refer to as BL.

THE MANAGERIAL IMPLICATIONS OF BRAND LOYALTY

At the outset of this chapter we outlined four principal management objectives with respect to RPB. These were to increase the presence of RPB for Brand A, to stimulate the consumption rate of Brand A purchasers engaging in RPB, to decrease the amount of RPB with respect to competing brands, and finally, to inoculate Brand A repeat buyers against brand switching. Attainment of these objectives was viewed as contributing significantly to the overall growth of market share.

Although the direct control of RPB seems (at least for now) out of reach, we have suggested a compromise. Instead of accepting the argument that chance factors

govern all of buyer behavior, we have divided RPB into
two portions, a stochastic and a deterministic portion,
and have labeled the latter BL. Having done so, we can
now recast the managerial objectives in terms of this
more limited (yet substantially more manageable) form of
buyer behavior.

The major implications of this line of reasoning are
twofold: first, it places squarely in management's lap the
ability to accomplish the aforementioned objectives and,
second, it focuses management's efforts on specific underlying deterministic processes. As described in later
chapters, we believe these are primarily psychological
(e.g., beliefs, attitudes, and intentions to repurchase).
Although psychology continues to address the influence
of such processes on behavior in nonconsumer contexts
(cf. Insko, 1967; Kiesler, Collins, and Miller, 1969; Fishbein and Ajzen, 1975), marketing researchers will have to
extend and, in some cases, substantially reformulate this
work to meet marketing's applied objectives. Isolated efforts in this direction (cf. Jacoby, 1971b; Reynolds,
Darden, and Martin, 1974; Jarvis and Wilcox, 1976) have
already been made, but continued progress hinges on one
fundamental issue: satisfactory BL measurement. Before
being able to acquire a firm grasp on and influence over
BL, the marketing manager must be able to measure and
monitor its existence adequately. It is this issue of
measurement to which most of this volume is directed.

TWO

TRENDS IN

Brand Loyalty Measurement:

A HISTORICAL PERSPECTIVE

A chronological review of the literature has three advantages. First, it can indicate the progress (or lack of progress) in the sophistication with which we have approached measurement. Second, it can identify the emergence of conflicting viewpoints and suggest potential resolutions. Finally, it can lead to predictions regarding the future of brand loyalty (BL) in marketing management, noting problems and recommending specific courses of action.

Before we enter into this account, a conceptual framework (beyond just that of chronology) is necessary. The measurement of BL has long been characterized by a variety of operational definitions. If management is ever to sort through this variety and arrive at informed decisions regarding the relative utility of individual measures, an attempt must be made to provide some

7

common basis for contrast and comparison. Normally, one might expect theory (i.e., a conceptual understanding of BL itself) to provide such a basis. This is unfortunately not the case. "The concept of brand loyalty has been defined by most researchers empirically instead of theoretically, a few researchers have stated that the empirical definition of brand loyalty *is* the theoretical definition" (Woodside and Clokey, 1975, p. 175). This bias toward empirics has created an important role for certain assumptions about measurement. Two, in particular, are worth noting and are described here as a conceptual framework for ordering the existing definitions.

The first assumption concerns the *level* at which BL is measured. By level, we refer simply to the number of consumers associated with a numerical observation. Two levels have dominated marketing research (cf. Bass, 1974): the individual (or "micro") and the aggregate (or "macro").

The individual level assumes that BL exists and can be measured for each consumer. Understandably, it is closely linked with what we have termed a deterministic philosophy. Purchasing, it is argued, is the output of a dynamic, decision-making system involving numerous psychological variables, and since BL is one of these variables, it should be placed in the context of the individual's process of cognitive/behavioral activities. A numerical aggregation over different individuals would only obscure this context and inhibit an understanding of the system.

The aggregate level assumes that BL exists and can be measured across some number of consumers. Reynolds and Wells (1977, p. 341), for example, describe an index of "repeat-purchase rate" that is arrived at by inspecting the total purchasing of one brand over a series of two-week intervals. The numerical observation in this case is based on the behavior of the entire sample. Little emphasis is placed on the understanding of any one purchase. Instead, the primary objective is heuristic— one of forecasting or predicting gross market phenomena such as brand share. Measures of this type have swayed more to the stochastic view of purchase behavior.

Beyond just the level at which BL is measured, empirical definitions have resorted to a second assumption. This concerns the *type* of data employed (i.e., the very nature of what is to be measured). Torgerson (1958, p. 14) points out that measurement must focus on some observable property. But what is the property underlying BL?

Three distinct answers to this question have emerged. The first stresses behavior, BL being the property of consistent repurchase of the same brand over time. This assumption restricts the empirical data base to observations regarding the outcomes of decision and ignores the cognitive processes which underlie and create those outcomes. The second answer stresses attitudes, BL being the property of psychological commitment (i.e., the beliefs, feelings, and intentions) that results in the consistent repurchase of the same brand over time. This assumption focuses measurement on elements involved in the cognitive process of decision, ignoring the behavioral outcome. Finally, a third answer stresses both behavioral and attitudinal properties. This composite view of BL attempts to define some statistical compromise that (advocates contend) addresses the true multivariate complexity of the construct.

To review, the diversity of BL measures is great. This generates a need for a conceptual framework with which to order and then evaluate the literature. Given the empirical bias of most investigators, one useful basis for a framework can be derived from the assumptions common to the actual measurement procedures. Specifically, two assumptions are often made. These concern the level (i.e., individual/micro or aggregate/macro) and type (i.e., behavioral, attitudinal, or composite) of data to be examined. In the chronological account to follow, we attempt to trace the development of these assumptions and summarize the current status of their associated measures.

BRAND LOYALTY MEASURES: 1923–1976

The study of brand loyalty did not begin, as previous reviews suggest, with George Brown and the *Chicago Tribune* panel of the 1950s. In the marketing literature alone, articles on the subject can be traced back to the early twenties. Copeland (1923), although he did not specifically use the term *loyalty,* described a phenomenon he labeled "brand insistence." Hypothesizing an attitudinal continuum stretching from recognition, through degrees of preference, to insistence, Copeland appears to be the first to suggest that an extreme attitude toward a particular brand might have a special effect on buyer behavior. Operationally, he proposed an exclusive purchase criterion and, thus, foreshadowed Brown's (1952) definition of "undivided loyalty."

Copeland's theorizing had, however, little apparent effect on research and thinking. The first empirical investigations to focus on something like BL did not appear until some 10 years later, when, in 1932, the Psychological Corporation began coordinating a survey of some 1500 different brands. The goal of this survey was to provide a statistical monitoring of market share. The business community appeared to have been receptive, and, by 1938, a total of some 50 universities were collecting data.

Some investigators (Link, 1934; Jenkins, 1938) became interested solely in the methodology of this survey: "the development of statistically reliable measures of people's changing buying habits is itself a project of major importance" (Link, 1934, p. 18). The procedure used in the survey was simply to ask the consumer to recall the last brand purchased. As Guest (1942) pointed out, this was really not much different from asking the consumer what he usually purchased. "In measuring the brand preferences of this group, trends could be established as accurately from the last purchase questions as from the usual purchase questions" (p. 186). Without explicitly recognizing their involvement, psychologists had begun their inquiry into repeat purchase behavior (RPB).

A major alternative to the questionnaire approach was proposed by Churchill (1942). Advocating the use of consumer panels, he contended that BL "can be measured only by watching everything that goes into the pantries of a fixed group of consumers" (p. 24). This type of control would allow the marketer to ask certain questions. From which brands am I obtaining customers? Once I have obtained them, are they staying with me (i.e., are they buying my brand exclusively)? Finally, if they are switching, which brands are they switching to? Churchill's approach toward BL was both behavioral and macro. It established a detailed aggregate statistical analysis of market share as a means of measuring BL.

Churchill's criterion was not, however, long in finding a rival. Guest (1944), adopting a viewpoint similar to Copeland's emphasis on attitudes, defined BL as "constancy of preference over a period of years in the life of the individual" (p. 17). Testing a large sample of children between 7 to 18 years of age, he contended that attitudes formed during childhood would be indicative of later purchase behavior. Guest's investigation was the first attempt to seek a micro model explanation of why consistency in consumer behavior appears in the market. Further, it provided empirical support for the status of attitudes as one of the prime determinants of BL.

Early work on BL was not, however, entirely methodological. McGregor (1940), for example, was one of the first to notice the importance of a relationship between advertising and BL. Separating consumers into the "shifters" and the "loyal" users, he suggested that advertising employ strategies geared specifically toward converting the brand switcher into the loyal customer.

Although thinking and research had already been devoted to BL for some 30 years, it was not until Brown's articles in 1952 and 1953 that the subject received widespread exposure and began generating substantial interest. Brown characterized an interesting mixture of both attitudinal and behavioral approaches. He viewed BL as representing "a deliberate decision to concentrate purchase on a single brand due to some real or imaginary superiority of that brand" (1953, p. 32). Yet, instead of investigating a person's attribution of superiority or the "deliberate" decision process of loyal buying, Brown became caught up in the measurement of loyalty via sequence-of-purchase operational definitions. Like Churchill, he viewed loyalty solely in terms of purchase records from a consumer panel. Unlike Churchill, and in contrast to the unibrand character of his definition, Brown recognized other types of loyalty besides the consistent purchasing of only one brand *(AAAAAA)*. He defined "divided loyalty" as the brand sequence of *ABABAB* (i.e., an alternation between two brands) and "unstable loyalty" as the brand sequence of *AAABBB* or the consistent buying of first one and then another brand. These new types of loyalty found meaning only through consideration of a sequence of behavior. Brown did little to isolate the factors that might be influential in determining such types of loyalty, nor did he accommodate for irregular sequences (e.g., *ABBACDB*).

Stimulated by, yet dissatisfied with, Brown's sequence-of-purchase analysis, Cunningham (1956a) proposed a new measure of BL. This was the "market-share concept," or the proportion-of-purchase index. Loyalty, from Cunningham's viewpoint, was nothing more nor less than "the proportion of total purchases represented by the largest single brand used" (p. 118). If Brand *X* received 65% of a family's purchases, then that family (or individual) was considered loyal to Brand *X,* and the percentage served as an index of the strength of that loyalty. The advantage of this measure was that it generated numerical values for each brand within the market. Thus, Cunningham could investigate such issues as "dual-brand loyalty," that is, the cumulative percentage of the two most frequently purchased brands. A major disadvantage was, however, that an arbitrary cutoff point by which to define the presence of loyalty had to be established. Typically, if a family allocated 50% or more of its purchases to a single brand, it was said to be loyal to that brand. But what of the case where a family split its purchases in equal thirds among three brands (e.g., Shell, Texaco, and Exxon) out of the larger set of available brands?

Besides the proportion-of-purchase criterion, Cunningham also considered a lost-gained ratio measure (where the brand with the lowest ratio of lost to gained customers was defined as having the most loyalty) and a number of sequence-of-purchase measures (of the variety used by Churchill and Brown). He concluded, however, that such measures (at least in comparison to the market-share concept) were excessively arbitrary.

The tendency in the 1950s to measure BL through panel data was challenged by Pessemier (1959). Using a laboratory simulation of shopping behavior, he created a situation in which the price of the most preferred brand (MPB) was steadily increased (or the prices of the other brands were all steadily decreased) on each of 10 consecutive purchase occasions. This price-until-switching measure of BL focused on more than just the behavior of switching; it focused on the number of price increases necessary to induce switching. If one conceives of loyalty as a drive state motivating the consumer to obtain a certain brand, Pessemier can be said to have asked how much negative reinforcement the consumer is willing to incur in the satisfaction of his drive. The shift in focus here is from considering *whether* brand loyalty exists to considering the *degree* (i.e., strength) to which it does exist. The all-or-none conceptualization is thus replaced by a continuum.

Pessemier's impact on BL measurement was, however, negligible in comparison with two other investigations that appeared at approximately the same time. One paper was in the form of a dissertation by Kuehn (1958). Building on mathematical advances in psychological learning theory, it proposed the initial version of what is called the linear-learning model of BL. The second paper was an address to the annual conference of the Advertising Research Foundation (ARF) by Lipstein (1959), in which he outlined the applications of a Markov process to the study of BL and brand switching. Both Lipstein and Kuehn were interested in applying stochastic processes (i.e., probability-of-purchase models) to the study and prediction of consumer behavior. The success of their research and ideas in the early sixties described the growth of what were essentially behavior-oriented, macro models of BL measurement.*

In the four-year period immediately following Lipstein's ARF address (1959–1963), a number of articles appeared on stochastic modeling. Common to all was the assumption that BL could be observed only in terms of the aggregation of sequence-of-purchase data from consumer panels. As stated by Lipstein:

> The observable manifestations of consumer loyalty or disloyalty are the sequence of consumer purchases . . . however, single consumers convey very little information about the market structure. For the sequencing to take on real meaning we must aggregate it over a reasonable sample of the population (1959, p. 102).

*One class of research not fully explored in the present review concerns the mathematical modeling of RPB. Typically, such modeling does not attempt to measure (i.e., operationally define) BL in the real world. As in the case of Ehrenberg's NBD/LSD theory (cf. Ehrenberg, 1971), it assumes a distribution function that, given certain market parameters, predicts the magnitude of repeat purchase. The Markov Chain analysis of BL (e.g., Lipstein, 1959) is an exception in that it requires the initial input of sales statistics. After such statistics have been entered into the analysis, they are transformed by matrix operations to give a predicted market share at some time in the future. Since our primary interest lies in real-world measurement of BL, only those models including some operational definition of the construct are discussed.

Until Lipstein, behavioral measures (such as those of Brown and Cunningham) had enabled investigators to obtain numerical values for each family. With the advent of stochastic models and their emphasis on market structure, BL measures began to reflect entire samples of consumers. Lipstein, for example, proposed two indices of BL: the probability of repurchase and the average staying time with the brand.

If we imagine a matrix of transition probabilities, each entry being the probability of a consumer's purchasing a brand k at time 2, given that he had purchased brand i at time 1, the main diagonal of this matrix can be said to represent the probability of repurchasing the initial brand chosen. All entries off the main diagonal represent, therefore, the chances of brand switching.

Lipstein worked with these probabilities as an index of BL but preferred the use of an average-staying-time measure. "This measure is very easily computed from the simple formula, one, divided by the probability of leaving the brand" (1959, p. 105). In this manner it predicted the average sequence length of a consumer's purchasing only one brand.

In the application of such matrices Lipstein found it useful to resort to an individual-difference model. He would divide his sample into two subpopulations: the "hard-core" buyers and the brand switchers. Somewhat along the line of Cunningham's strategy, "hard-core" buyers were defined as families concentrating 75% or more of their purchases on only one brand (Harary and Lipstein, 1962, p. 32). In effect the loyal buyers were separated out by a proportion-of-purchase criterion so that their probabilities would not bias the larger group of homogeneous brand switchers.

Lipstein's transition probabilities were not the only viable stochastic measures of BL. Frank (1962), working from Kuehn's premise of a linear-learning model, investigated the "repeat purchase probability" and the "return purchase probability":

given that a customer has made a run of 1, 2, 3, . . ., n purchases of a certain brand, what is the relative frequency of buying the same brand at next purchase. . . . This relationship is looked at in two ways: first, as a measure of the extent to which a customer's brand choices in the immediate past can be used to predict the next choice; second, as a measure of the extent of habitual purchasing behavior (Frank, 1962, p. 44).

Instead of a "loyalty" conceptualization Frank sought to emphasize repeat-purchase probability as habit. Ehrenberg (1964) thought this somewhat simplistic but nevertheless useful. Kuehn and Day (1964) actually saw the repeat-purchase probability as an improvement on old behavioral measures of BL. "When the expected behavior of an individual is viewed as a set of probabilities related to available brands, a richer and more flexible concept of 'brand loyalty' is provided" (p. 31).

Not all investigators, however, shared this emphasis on probabilities. Although the application of stochastic models was certainly dominant during the early sixties, alternative approaches toward measuring BL were being proposed. Farley (1964a), for example, investigated an economic explanation of loyalty and developed two new measures. These were termed: N_{ar} (number of brands bought by family r during one year) and S_{ar} (a statistic taking on the value 1 if the family's favorite brand changed halfway through the year, and the value 0 if it did not). Note that the second measure was close to being a short-term version of Guest's time-preference measure. These indices were subsequently changed by Farley (1964b) into N_m (the average number of brands bought by families that purchase Brand m) and S_m (the percentage of families in the market that change their MPB halfway through the year). This alteration reflected a shift away from measures at the micro or individual level (N_{ar} and S_{ar}) to market-structure statistics (N_m and S_m). Brand loyalties were assumed to be greater, the lower the value of these statistics.

Dommermuth (1965) proposed an interesting measure that apparently has had little application in the marketing literature. Crossing the number of stores shopped at with the number of brands considered, he developed a matrix in which certain cells reflect specific buying strategies. Subjects were asked to indicate (usually for a durable product) how many stores they would visit and on the average how many brands in each store they would consider before reaching a final purchase decision. If their responses fell in the matrix cell indicating a large number of stores but relatively few brands in each store, Dommermuth concluded that they were highly loyal purchasers.

Tucker (1964) went back to a combination of the measures first proposed by Brown and Pessemier. Asserting that a subject's behavior was "the full statement of what brand loyalty is" (p. 32), Tucker relied on the sequence-of-purchase criterion (e.g., three or more consecutive purchases of the same brand) to define the existence of BL. (This "three consecutive purchases" criterion was again popularized by McConnell in 1968a.) To determine the *strength* of this behavior, however, Tucker proposed a premium measure á là Pessemier (1959). After a subject had made three successive choices of the same brand, a penny was placed on the brand that she had rarely, if at all, chosen. The addition of more pennies onto this least preferred brand continued until the subject was induced to switch.

This tendency to combine behavioral and attitudinal indices of BL soon came to have influence on other investigators. The late sixties were characterized by a drop in the popularity of stochastic models (at least with respect to BL) and an increasing stress on loyalty as something more than simply RPB.

Cunningham (1967) reflected this trend by developing a measure of "perceived brand commitment." The basis for this index was the subject's verbal report of his likely behavior upon being confronted with his favorite brand's being out of stock. From this information Cunningham

separated consumers into those with high, low, and ambiguous loyalty. The highly brand-loyal consumer was
one who stated a consistency of purchasing with respect
to a certain brand and indicated that, if this brand were
out of stock, he would either wait until another shopping
trip or go to another store to make his purchase of this
brand.

Sheth (1968) recognized the value of stochastic
models but at the same time emphasized the limitations
inherent in a macro approach toward BL. "What we
need is a model that will, besides aggregate brand loyalty
measures, provide measures of each consumer's brand
loyalty" (p. 395). As many investigators did before him,
Sheth saw loyalty primarily in terms of behavior. In
contrast, however, to prior research, he sought a statistical combination of two important behavioral criteria:
proportion of purchase and sequence of purchase.

He accomplished this goal in a factor analytic model
of BL. As explained in some detail by Howard and Sheth
(1969), it was reasoned that a factor score represented "a
linear combination of the observed purchase behavior on
a series of trials . . . based on both the frequency of
purchase of a brand and the pattern of these purchases"
(p. 249). Sheth (1970) made the logical extension of this
model to the multidimensional case. As in the earlier
papers "multidimensional loyalty scores are essentially
frequencies weighted by degree of switching" (p. 353).

Massy, Frank, and Lodahl (1968), in a factor analysis
of buying behavior, proposed a similar method of BL
measurement. In their solution, store loyalty and BL
combined to account for as much as 70% of the overall
variance of the panel's purchasing records. Statistics
loading positively on the BL factor were average length
of brand runs and market share. This tendency to merge
sequence with proportion measures reaffirmed Sheth's
factor analytic model. Such factor solutions are,
however, greatly restricted by their input. Massy, Frank,
and Lodahl, by considering only a limited number of behavioral indices, impaired the generality of their findings.

Day (1969) challenged such behavioral measures, arguing that they reflected a great deal of "spurious loyalty." Like Cunningham, he saw the truly loyal customer as one consistent in both behavior and attitude.

> Loyal segment is often defined as a buyer who devotes at least 50% of his product purchase to a single brand. In this study, 108 of 148 buyers would be classified as brand loyal on that basis. However, if loyal buyers were required to have an extremely favorable initial attitude toward the brand as well as buying the brand on a majority of occasions, then the brand loyal segment is reduced to 76 buyers (p. 31).

Almost all the measurement techniques described thus far would have failed to identify the 32 behaviorally consistent but attitudinally nonloyal consumers found in this study. Day's argument was, therefore, that ordinary behavioral measures overrepresented the existence of BL. To improve the accuracy of assessment, he proposed a loyalty index (L_i) that was a function of both the proportion of purchases $(P[B_i])$ and the attitude toward the brand (A_i). True or "intentional loyalty" was thus assessed by having consumers satisfy *both* a behavioral and an attitudinal criterion.

Up to this point, measures of BL were either behavioral or composite (i.e., behavioral combined with attitudinal). With the exception of the work of Copeland (1923) and Guest (1944, 1955, 1964), which had relatively little impact, investigators viewed brand-loyal attitudes as mere refinements on the central criterion of consistency of purchase. Regardless of whether a micro or a macro interpretation of human behavior was employed, these approaches failed to distinguish between brand-loyal behavior and brand-loyal attitudes. Such a distinction was advanced by Jacoby (1969, 1970, 1971b; Jacoby and Olson, 1970). "Brand loyal behavior is defined as the overt act of selective repeat purchasing based on evaluative psychological decision processes, while brand loyal attitudes are the underlying predispositions to behave in such a selective fashion" (p. 26, 1971b). Jacoby contended it would probably be worthwhile to study the underlying brand-loyal attitudes, not as an adjunct to behavior, but in their own right because they were most likely the causative link capable of providing an understanding of the reasons for and strength of behavioral BL.

Using Sherif's attitudinal-change model of assimilation-contrast (Sherif and Hovland, 1961; Sherif, Sherif, and Nebergall, 1965; Sherif and Sherif, 1967), Jacoby hypothesized three general regions along a single continuum of brand preference. If one were to scale the consumer's attitudes toward the brands he considered as purchase alternatives, there would be some accepted (i.e., preferred) brands, a few neutral brands, and a number of rejected or disliked brands. Jacoby based his indices of the strength of BL on the respective sizes of these regions, the number of brands within them, and the distances between regions.

> The strength of brand loyalty is a function of the distance between regions. Loyalty is stronger the greater the difference between the regions of acceptance and rejection, and between the regions of acceptance and neutrality. . . . The strength of brand loyalty will, to some extent, also be a function of the ratio between the number of brands in the regions of acceptance and rejection. Loyalty becomes stronger as the proportion of brands in the rejection region increases while the proportion of brands in the acceptance region decreases (1971b, p. 28).

A revision of the proportion measure, cited by Bennett and Kassarjian (1972), entails an extension of the R/A ratio (i.e., the number of brands in the rejected region divided by the number of brands in the accepted region) to include the neutral scalings. Mathematically, it appeared as brand loyalty = R/A $(1.0 - NC)$, where NC

denotes the neutral or noncommitment region and all parameters are expressed as proportions of the total number of brands.

Speller (1973) reinforced the argument of a relationship between attitudinal factors and BL by finding that intention and attitude measures were strongly correlated with subsequent proportion-of-purchase data. Out of the seven products involved in his study, six evidenced this tendency.

Anderson (1974) has taken the unusual step of extending an interest in attitudes to the macro level of measurement, accomplishing this by partitioning sales into two orthogonal components: preference-oriented $(1 - \theta)$ and random (θ) purchasing. The regression coefficient θ is solved via a prediction of a given brand's sales from the shelf space devoted to the brand. The resultant index $(1 - \theta)m$, where m is the sample size, reflects the number of people who are not influenced by shelf space and who, according to Anderson, are brand loyal in their purchasing. Unfortunately, Anderson did not establish the validity of this approach (i.e., whether or not shelf space really can estimate attitudes). Given the behavioral nature of its data base and the arbitrariness of its assumptions, it would seem better at present to classify Anderson's index as behavioral rather than truly attitudinal or even composite.

Reynolds, Darden, and Martin (1974), returning to the individual or micro level of measurement, propose a traditional psychometric approach toward attitudes, namely, scale construction. Although based on an analysis of store-related attitudes, their operational definition is viewed primarily within the context of "consumer loyalty" (i.e., store loyalty as one part of a multidimensional construct).

Their scaling procedure begins with an a priori set of four statements conceived to reflect a self-designation of store-loyal behavior: for example, "I do most of my shopping in the same stores I have always shopped in." These statements are positioned in a 144-item psychographic questionnaire. Item ratings are recorded on a forced-choice, agree-versus-disagree Likert format. A principal component analysis using a varimax rotation was then performed on the data. It isolated all four store loyalty items on the same component (individual loadings ranging from .52 to .63 on a sample of 304). The authors conclude that "given the relatively high factor loadings and subsample stability, the scale appears to have sufficient construct validity and to represent a generalized dimension of store loyalty" (p. 78). Item responses can thus be summated and a total store loyalty score (ranging from 4 to 24) considered.

In a similar vein Monroe and Guiltinan (1975) use a one-item scaling to assess an attitudinal trade-off between brand name and price. Although not explicitly linked to a measurement of BL, their operationalization is at the very least suggestive: "I make my purchase selection according to my favorite brand name, regardless of price."

A more direct attempt at BL measurement is reflected in a paper by Jarvis and Wilcox (1976). Returning to the procedures originally advocated by Jacoby (1969), they consider an index of "cognitive loyalty." The attempt is noteworthy in that it goes beyond brand preference to brand awareness. Specifically, the R/A ratio is corrected by the addition of a term dependent "on the number of brands available within the community" (p. 151). This facilitates a comparison of measures across different consumer segments and product categories. A possibility not explored in this approach would be to define awareness from a psychological perspective (e.g., an independent measurement of evoked set).

Finally, Jacoby, Jones, and Chestnut (in preparation) are exploring an attitudinal measurement suggested by Juster's (1966) "purchase probability scale." This scale requires subjects to indicate their likelihood of purchase of each available brand in terms of 11 probability statements: the chances of buying Brand X are . . . 99 in 100,

9 in 10, 8 in 10, . . . 1 in 10, and 1 in 100. Empirical results adduced by Juster (1966) and Gruber (1970) seem to support the scale's increased sensitivity and predictive validity with regard to the purchase of nondurable goods.

In terms of BL the purchase probability scale provides an opportunity to classify zones of brand acceptance, neutrality, and rejection. Attitudes are usually defined as having three primary components: affect, cognition, and behavioral predisposition. Given that a probability statement of intent to purchase reflects a behavioral predisposition to buy, data collected with the purchase probability scale are considered attitudinal and are being used to develop new measures of BL. For example, if a consumer rates a number of brands along the probability scale, the nature of the resultant distribution of brands (e.g., the number of probability intervals without brand assignment, the distance between probability intervals with brand assignments, the number of brands that cluster together, the skew of the distribution, along with a variety of other factors) reflects how differentiated or complex the consumer is in terms of his brand-related attitudes. The purchase probability scale should provide a more valid and sensitive scaling of attitudinal acceptance-neutrality-rejection regions along a general continuum reflecting behavior predispositions toward branded products.

Although the popularity of the attitudinal approach toward BL has grown, the older behavioral and composite indices have continued to be reworked in the hope of providing better measurement. With regard to purely behavioral operationalizations, Carman's (1970) entropy measure is a case in point. Carman defines a loyalty index "θ" equal to negative the summation of p_i multiplied by the log of p_i, where p_i is nothing more than the proportion of purchases going to a given brand. Carman's index differentiates itself from Cunningham's (1956a) only by making certain assumptions about buying behavior. It is still not clear, however, exactly whether or how this measure is better than other indices.

Another example is that of the loyalty index proposed by Burford, Enis, and Paul (1971). Instead of weighting behavioral statistics through a factor analytic model, these authors combined factors such as brand switching, number of brands available, and store loyalty through a process of aggregating via a geometric mean. They provide some evidence that the resultant index of BL yields both "reasonable and meaningful" results.

Brown (1972) takes a somewhat different approach toward purchase behavior in an index referred to as "private brand loyalty." The attempt here is to measure the number of different product categories (from a set of seven frequently purchased nondurables) in which private-label brands are purchased. It is this number of products (i.e., the breadth over which private labels are acquired), and not the consistent purchasing of any one brand, that defines the degree of loyalty. Four somewhat arbitrary degrees are considered: disloyalty (zero or one product), semidisloyalty (two or three products), semiloyalty (four or five products), and loyalty (six or seven products).

Following this example of defining a "new" type of loyalty behavior, Bubb and van Rest (1973), building on earlier research by Wind (1970), suggest an index of industrial "source loyalty." The conceptual approach underlying this definition is unusual. For lack of a better label, we have referred to it as an estimate by elimination. The assumption is that "loyalty will account for the residual tendency to buy from a previously favoured supplier, when each other factor has been isolated and accounted for" (p. 26). As the authors themselves note, this is a rather "catchall" perspective, one bound to vary greatly with the circumstances surrounding purchase. Its contention is, however, interesting in that any variance predictive of repurchase but not related to the more rational aspects of decision (i.e., price, product qualities, etc.) may be equated to the influence of loyalty.

Livesy (1973) resorts to a less controversial measurement (the traditional probability of repurchase) but, like

Bubb and van Rest, places loyalty in a unique purchasing context. The context is that of rental agreements: "brand loyalty is here defined in terms of the propensity of a consumer to renew his rental agreement month by month and year by year. This definition is qualified below by reference to the reason for termination and the nature of the choice made by the subscriber who terminates" (p. 219). Specifically, only those renters switching to another make of the product (i.e., not just discontinuing service) were considered disloyal.

Fry et al. (1973) have proposed what seems to be the first behavioral measure to assess the longitudinal characteristics of rather long time intervals. Their measurement approach stems from the analysis of bank account records covering several decades. Bank loyalty, expressed as the difference between the conditional probability of a consumer's having an account at time t_1 (given that he had an account at the same branch at time t_{n-1}) and the unconditional probability of a consumer's having an account at time t_1, offers a special opportunity to consider the influence of early experience on brand loyalty. Much like Guest in the early 1940s Fry et al. conclude that stable loyalty patterns are developed at an early age and are carried over into adult life. "A final note of some interest is that parental influence remains a factor of significance through the entire pattern . . ." (p. 521).

In contrast to these measures of private, source, rental, and bank loyalty, McCann (1974), returning to the more traditional BL construct, suggests a variant of Cunningham's (1956) dual- and triple-brand loyalty. The index, termed FRA, "measures the fraction of the total product quantity purchased by the household that can be accounted for by the purchases of the five brands that are purchased most by the family" (p. 403). As McCann points out, this is simply the accumulation of the top five market shares for each family. Loyalty is then defined as a dichotomous variable based on the mean of FRA. Loyal purchasers have an index greater than the mean (i.e., approaching 1.0), while disloyal purchasers have an index less than the mean.

Dupuy (1975) focuses on a special case of the bank loyalty measure of Fry et al. Examining the shopping behavior of "new residents," he proposes a loyalty measure based on changes in bank/store affiliation resulting from the move to a new community. Given that they have the option, loyal consumers are those that maintain the same affiliation.

Most recently, behavioral indices have stressed the proportion-of-purchase criterion. Charlton and Ehrenberg (1976) impose what might be referred to as a 2/3 index of brand loyalty. "Mutually exclusive groups of 'loyal' users of a brand of tea have been defined as those buying a brand four or more times in a certain 6-week period that was free of marketing activity" (p. 158). This seems to compromise between the standard 50% market share criterion and Lipstein's more restrictive "hardcore" segmentation.

Nordstrom and Swan (1976) talk of a similar measure in their consideration of dealer/agency loyalty in the purchase of cars. Consumers are said to be loyal to a dealer if they show evidence of having made two or more purchases from the same dealer. If we assume a relatively long mean interpurchase interval, this amounts to what is in many cases a high proportion of the purchases.

Composite measures have not developed in as great a number as the behavioral measures, but they have demonstrated a good deal more sophistication. One of the more interesting approaches is that proposed by Newman and Werbel (1973). Intended primarily for the assessment of BL in the purchase of durable goods, this measure resembles Cunningham's (1967) perceived-commitment index. Instead of asking for an "out-of-stock" decision, however, Newman and Werbel chose to concentrate on information search tendencies. The measure consists of asking a series of questions and assigning varying strengths of BL to differing patterns of response. The highest score can be obtained by a customer who has: (1) repurchased the old brand, (2) thought mainly of the old brand at the outset of his decision process, and (3) did not seek any product-related information. According to this operationalization, a brand-loyal consumer is consistent in his behavior, unibrand directed in his decision, and restrictive in his information search activities.

Lutz and Winn (1975) take a somewhat different but no less complicated direction. Their objective is to improve the composite of overt purchase behavior and brand attitude first suggested by Day (1969). To do this, they propose an equation that makes use of a basic tenet of Bayesian multivariate analysis. In combining two statistical estimates, greater weight should be allocated to the more "precise" information. In terms of a BL measure, the result is an index constructed so that "the estimate (i.e., attitude or behavior) with the smaller variance will receive more weight in determining the 'posterior' loyalty score for each consumer" (p. 105). A preliminary comparison of this index with other operationalizations does seem to provide "acceptable" levels of both convergent and discriminant validity.

Bellenger, Steinberg, and Stanton (1976) define store loyalty in terms of a composite of estimates but do not use any assumptions regarding statistical precision. They offer instead a more simplified approach toward combining measures of proportion of shopping, store preference, and store purchasing intention. Unfortunately, few data are provided, either from theory or empirics, that might support such a combination.

Finally, in contrast to Newman and Werbel's positing of an overall decline in search behavior, Towle and Martin (1976) define a BL measure based on the direction of such search. Specifically, they relate loyalty to a tendency for acquiring the manufacturer's name from packaged goods. Although they rely on self-reports of behavior, this approach is suggestive of and might well be enhanced by one of the newer "process" methodologies described by Jacoby and Chestnut (in preparation).

SYNTHESIS AND TRENDS

The preceding review attempted to depict the various historical trends in BL measurement. It did so with three objectives in mind. These were to outline the general trends of BL research, the opposing viewpoints or philosophies, and the potential for future development.

As we suggested at the outset, and as our historical examination of the literature has reinforced, measures of BL have all shared certain fundamental assumptions. Two were highlighted in our review. These concerned the level and type of data examined. By way of summary Table 2.1 organizes and displays the various operational definitions by author in light of their particular assumptions. This table cites only those authors who first proposed some unique measurement of BL. As such, this compilation is not meant to reflect all BL research that subsequently used the definitions.

In terms of general progress the table evidences a gradual trend toward a more complex understanding of BL. It is quite apparent that the purely behavioral definitions have dominated the measurement of BL. More than half the studies mentioned have used actual purchase behavior (or self-reports of such behavior) as their central criterion. This domination appears to continue at present, becoming more diversified through positing "new" types of loyalty. Measures of rental, bank, store, source, and agency loyalty, for example, have greatly changed the overall meaning of the construct. Unfortunately, despite this increase in types of loyalty, little has been done to alter the basic emphasis on proportion or sequence of purchase.

As a counterpoint to this domination, however, both attitudinal and composite definitions have become increasingly more popular and varied. With the distinction between brand-loyal attitudes and brand-loyal behavior, a more viable approach toward understanding the underlying dynamics of loyalty has appeared. These measures no longer accept two successive purchases as

Table 2.1 ARTICLES THAT FIRST PROPOSED UNIQUE OPERATIONAL DEFINITIONS OF BL

Behavioral	Attitudinal	Composite
Macro		
Churchill (1942)		
Cunningham (1956a)		
Lipstein (1959)		
Frank (1962)		
Farley (1964a)		
Anderson (1974)		
Micro		
Copeland (1923)	Guest (1942)	Copeland (1923)
Brown (1952)	Guest (1955)	Pessemier (1959)
Cunningham (1956a)	Jacoby (1969)	
Farley (1964b)	Jacoby and Olson (1970)	Cunningham (1967)
Tucker (1964)	Bennett and Kassarjian (1972)	Day (1969)
Dommermuth (1965)	Reynolds et al. (1974)	Newman and Werbel (1973)
McConnell (1968a)	Monroe and Guiltinan (1975)	Lutz and Winn (1975)
Sheth (1968)	Jarvis and Wilcox (1976)	Bellenger et al. (1976)
Massy et al. (1968)	Jacoby et al. (in preparation)	Towle and Martin (1976)
Carman (1970)		
Burford et al. (1971)		
Brown (1972)		
Fry et al. (1973)		
Bubb and van Rest (1973)		
Livesy (1973)		
McCann (1974)		
Dupuy (1975)		
Charlton and Ehrenberg (1976)		
Nordstrom and Swan (1976)		

sufficient for denoting BL. Instead they have begun to seek a deeper theory (in terms of the causative psychological constructs) of behavioral consistency. In terms of measurement capability and actual understanding of the phenomenon, this trend seems to offer a great deal more than the early, strictly behavioral orientation does.

With this emphasis on BL as something more than just behavior, investigators have made increasing use of the micro assumption and its accompanying deterministic philosophy of research. Given a gradual realization that the complexities of market share can never be adequately understood unless the individual roots of such purchase behavior are made explicit, the mathematical modeling of aggregate behavioral data has lost a considerable amount of its appeal. Witness the fact that, of the several BL indices proposed since 1970, only one (i.e., Anderson, 1974) has been directed at measuring the entire market, and even this definition has stressed an attitudinal interpretation. The conflict between micro versus macro levels of measurement appears, therefore, at least for the present, to have resolved itself in favor of a more individualistic analysis.

What effects have these trends had for the course and future potential of BL research? To explore this issue, we conducted an analysis of the available references on RPB in terms of the number of articles published per five-year blocks of time from 1940 to 1974 (see Figure 2.1 and Table 2.2). The solid line in Figure 2.1 represents the total number of articles that have, in some general way, concerned themselves with BL. The broken line represents the number of articles published that have had the term *brand loyalty* (or close equivalent) in their title and, thus, probably reflect a more specific focus.

Two conclusions can be reached from a consideration of these data. First, it is readily apparent that the bulk of relevant literature has accumulated within the past 15 years. Second, if one can assume that the term *brand loyalty* in the title actually does represent greater atten-

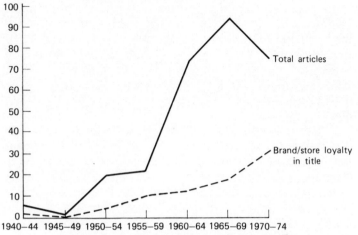

Figure 2.1   Trend of brand loyalty research.

tion's being given to the construct per se, then BL research has steadily become more focused. One might contend that research in the area is growing and, in the process, substantially increasing in its sophistication.

In summary the present status of BL research can be characterized as that of a construct undergoing substantial revision and redirection in measurement orientation. From an overly behavioral, macro approach,

Table 2.2   ANALYSIS OF BL ARTICLES BY 5-YEAR INTERVALS

Years	Total Articles	Brand/Store Loyalty in Title
Before 1940	3	0
1940–1944	5	2
1945–1949	1	0
1950–1954	19	3
1955–1959	22	9
1960–1964	73	12
1965–1969	95	18
1970–1974	85	36
N	303	80

it is gradually making the transition to a more micro understanding of the attitudinal and cognitive mechanisms underlying choice behavior. Unfortunately, this redefinition has placed much of the previously reported "findings" regarding BL in question. As will soon be documented, a majority of the research undertaken has been founded on highly suspect measurement techniques.

THREE

A COMPREHENSIVE REVIEW OF THE

Operational Definitions of Brand Loyalty

Nearly six decades of marketing theory and research have been devoted to considering brand loyalty (BL). From the earliest paper on "brand insistence" (Copeland, 1923) to the present the relevance of this concept for understanding and predicting consumer purchase decisions has been universally acknowledged. It is, therefore, extremely interesting to find, upon reviewing this literature, that no one quite agrees on exactly what BL is.

Consider the fact that more than 50 different operational definitions have been employed in the hundreds of studies now available on BL. As our perspectives have changed, so has the measurement of BL. Unlike our viewpoints, however, measurement indices have rarely been critically reviewed or shaped into more sophisticated approximations. Once created, BL indices tend to remain in existence to provide a technical clutter of widely varying operational definitions. If meaningful progress is to be made, these definitions should be critically evaluated in terms of their adequacy. The "best" measures need to be identified and the others discarded.

The following review of loyalty measures was undertaken to meet these needs. For this review, the various operational measures have been placed into one of three categories: behavioral (i.e., those indices based on actual overt behavior or self-reports of actual past behavior), attitudinal (i.e., those based strictly on preference statements or statements of likely behavior), and composite (i.e., those reflecting some combination of behavioral and attitudinal aspects). In all, 53 different operational definitions are discussed.*

---

*If anything, this is a conservative estimate of the existing measures. In compiling our review, we have excluded the rather large unpublished (and generally proprietary) literature of marketing research. Our reasons for doing so are threefold. First, measures generated in this literature are not openly available to all. Second, when measures are described, the details of their administration are often unclear. Finally, in much of this research there is no way of ensuring the degree to which measures have been conceptually/empirically reviewed before implementation. At least with the academic literature editorial review and consensus can be assumed present. It is reassuring to note, however, that many of the measures included in this text obtain rather extensive use outside academia. One major syndicated service, for example, employs the information search operationalization described by Towle and Martin (1976). Numerous research projects of which the authors are aware have adopted one or another of the proportion of purchase criteria. In general, the similarity between basic and applied measurement techniques seems great.

BEHAVIORAL INDICES OF BRAND LOYALTY

More than 60% (33) of the 53 measures available are behavioral in orientation; that is, they are based either on the actual purchasing behavior of the consumer or on his report of that behavior. These indices can be further subdivided into five groups: (1) those concerned with proportion of purchases devoted to a given brand, (2) those concerned with the sequence in which brands are purchased, (3) those that reflect probability of purchase, (4) those that synthesize or seem to combine several behavioral criteria, and, finally, (5) a number of miscellaneous measures. The references cited with each index represent, as far as can be determined, the earliest published use of each.

Proportion-of-Purchase Measures

1. *Exclusive Purchase* (Copeland, 1923; Churchill, 1942; and Brown, 1952). Here BL is said to exist for a consumer when he repetitively purchases a single brand. This measure does not allow for any deviations; a consumer must purchase Brand A without exception.
2. *Market-Share Concept* (Cunningham 1956a, 1956b). Loyalty is defined in terms of the percentage of total purchases devoted to the single most frequently purchased brand. In many situations the buyer is said to be brand loyal when this percentage exceeds 50%.
3. *Hard-Core Criterion* (Lipstein, 1959). This is the same as the market-share concept (Number 2), except that it adopts a higher cutoff point of 75%.
4. *Two-Thirds Criterion* (Charlton and Ehrenberg, 1976). In an experimental simulation of brand choice, consumers are allowed a weekly selection of one of three different brands. "Loyal" users are defined as those "buying a brand four or more times in a certain 6-week period that

was free of marketing activity'' (p. 158). This is equivalent to a market-share measure with a cutoff of 67%.

5. *Dual Brand Loyalty* (Cunningham, 1956a, 1956b). Loyalty is defined in terms of the percentage of total purchases devoted to the two most frequently purchased brands.

6. *Triple Brand Loyalty* (Cunningham, 1956a, 1956b). Loyalty is defined in terms of the percentage of total purchases devoted to the three most frequently purchased brands.

7. *FRA* (McCann, 1974). An extension of triple brand loyalty, FRA is equated to the sum of the top five brand shares. Consumers are considered brand loyal if they score greater than the mean of this index.

Sequence-of-Purchase Measures

8. *Divided Loyalty* (Brown, 1952). This refers to a specific type of loyalty. It exists when the purchase sequence alternates between two brands (*A* and *B*) in the following manner: *ABABABAB,* and so on. Unfortunately, real-world purchase data rarely reflect such pure sequences.

9. *Unstable Loyalty* (Brown, 1952). This type of loyalty is defined to exist whenever a consumer consistently buys one brand for a period of time and then switches to consistently buying another brand (e.g., *AAABBB*).

10. *Three-in-a-Row Criterion* (Tucker, 1964; and McConnell, 1968a). Loyalty is said to exist for a brand whenever a sequence of three or more consecutive purchases of that brand is made.

11. *Number of Brand Runs* (Massy, Frank, and Lodahl, 1968). A brand run is defined as "any consecutive sequence of purchases of the same brand at one store . . . a run is terminated and a new one begun whenever the family changes its store or brand" (p. 20). Here BL is defined in degree (as opposed to presence or absence) and is inversely related to the number of brand runs. The lower the number of brand runs, the stronger the BL. Thus the

number of brand runs reflects a general tendency to switch.

12. *Average Length of Brand Runs* (Massy, Frank, and Lodahl, 1968). This is the average number of brands contained within a respondent's brand runs. The greater the magnitude of this index, the longer the runs, and thus, the greater the consistency of behavior. This measure makes no provision for an arbitrary cutoff point at which the consumer is considered to be either loyal or disloyal to a particular brand; that is, the definition is one of degree, not presence or absence.

Probability-of-Purchase Measures

13. *First-Order (Markov) Probability of Repurchase* (Lipstein, 1959). According to this operationalization, given a first-order stationary matrix of transition probabilities, the diagonal entries can be treated as indices of loyalty.

14. *Average Staying Time* (Lipstein, 1959). Given the first-order, stationary matrix of transition probabilities, one can predict the average number of purchases for which a consumer will stay with the brand in question by taking the reciprocal of the probability of switching from the brand.

15. *Repeat Purchase Probability* (Frank, 1962). Loyalty is here defined as the relative frequency of purchases devoted to a specific brand during a set of previous purchases.

16. *Return Purchase Probability* (Frank, 1962). On the assumption that a customer switched to another brand on some purchase trial $(1, 2, \ldots, n)$, the return purchase probability is defined by the relative frequency of returning to the first brand on the next $(n + 1)$ purchase trial.

17. $P(B_{t}|B_{t_{n-1}}) - P(B_{t})$ (Fry et al., 1973). This is a longitudinally based measure of bank loyalty defined as the difference between the conditional probability that a consumer will open an account at time t (given that he had opened an account at the same branch at a prior time

t_{n-1}) and the unconditional probability of a consumer's opening an account at that branch.

Synthesis Measures

18. *The Shopping Matrix* (Dommermuth, 1965). A p-by-p matrix is created, rows being the average number of brands looked at in a given store and columns being the number of stores visited. Subjects respond by indicating the cell in the matrix that reflects their own buying behavior for a specific product. Loyal consumers are those indicating a cell characterized by many stores but few brands per store.

19. *Sheth Factor Scores* (Sheth, 1968). These are proportion-of-purchase measures weighted by the sequence in which the brand was obtained. Scores are generated from a principal-components reduction of a matrix in which each vector is a sequence of brand purchases (an entry of 1 standing for the purchase of a given brand and an entry of 0 standing for the purchase of another brand).

20. *Massy, Frank, and Lodahl Factor Scores* (Massy, Frank, and Lodahl, 1968). Massy, Frank, and Lodahl propose a factor analytic combination of proportion-of-purchase data with average length of brand run that is similar to Sheth's factor scores.

21. *Loyalty Index* (Burford, Enis, and Paul, 1971). This measure is defined as:

$$L_i = 100 \left[b_i \cdot \frac{k + 1 - s_i}{m} \cdot \frac{n + 1 - p_i}{n} \right]^{1/3}$$

"where b_i = fraction of budget for the product class allocated to the loyalty object during the survey period by the ith consumer

s_i = number of switches from the loyalty object to some other store or brand during the survey period by the ith consumer

p_i = number of stores patronized or brands purchased by the ith consumer during the survey period

m = number of intervals in the survey period

$k = m - 1$ = number of opportunities to switch

n = number of stores or brands available to the consumer during the survey period

note: plus one is added to the numerators of the second and third ratios to prevent division into zero, which would result in an index of 0.0″ (p. 20).

22. *Entropy Measure, Theta, θ* (Carman, 1970). Loyalty is here defined as equal to negative the summation of p_i times the log of p_i, where p_i is the proportion of purchases devoted to brand i.

Miscellaneous Loyalty Measures

23. *Lost-Gained Ratio* (Cunningham, 1956a). Given data on purchases made at two points in time, the brand with the lowest ratio of lost-to-gained customers is said to have the greatest BL.

24. N_m (Farley, 1964a). Loyalty is here defined as the average number of brands bought by families of Brand m.

25. S_m (Farley, 1964a). This measure of loyalty is simply the percentage of families differing in their most preferred brand (MPB) from the first to the second halves of the year.

26. N_{ar} (Farley, 1964b). Loyalty is here defined as the number of brands within a product class purchased during a given period of time (e.g., one year) by a given family. Seggev (1970) renames this index "brand assortment" and shortens the time interval to 20 weeks.

27. S_{ar} (Farley, 1964b). This is a measure of MPB switching and takes on the value of 1 if the MPB during the second half of the year differs from that during the first half. If the MPB remains the same throughout the year, this index becomes 0.

28. $(1 - \theta)m$ (Anderson, 1974). This is a macro index of the number of people purchasing out of "brand allegiance." Instead of measuring such allegiance directly, Anderson takes behavioral data (i.e., sales) and, by a multiple regression, partials out the effect of "random" purchasing (operationally defined by the shelf space devoted to a given brand). Theta is merely the beta weight for the shelf-space predictor, and m is the sample size. $(1 - \theta)m$ is then assumed to index preference-oriented sales.

29. *Estimate by Elimination* (Bubb and van Rest, 1973). Loyalty is equated to the "residual" of unexplained variance in the prediction of consistent purchasing. "If loyalty is one of the factors which are considered in the buying decision, we can assess the behavior due to loyalty by separating out the other influences" (p. 26).

30. *Private-Brand Loyalty* (PBL) (Brown, 1972). A "private" brand is defined as "a product manufactured, packaged, and labeled for sale in a specific store or chain of stores" (p. 4). Consumers are considered loyal to private brands if they report purchasing such brands across a variety of different product categories. Categories include: canned vegetables, frozen vegetables, canned fruit, frozen food other than vegetables, dairy products, bakery preparations, and household cleanser products. Loyalty is divided into four levels.

PBL Level	Number of Product Categories in Which the Respondent Purchases Private Brands
Disloyal	0 or 1
Semidisloyal	2 or 3
Semiloyal	4 or 5
Loyal	6 or 7

31. *New-Resident Loyalty* (Dupuy, 1975). Loyalty is said to exist when, after a change in residence, the consumer allocates a majority of business to the same retailer. Data are presented on behavior toward banks and supermarkets.

32. *Dealer/Agency Loyalty* (Nordstrom and Swan, 1976). Consumers are considered loyal to a given automobile dealer if they report having made two or more purchases from the same dealer.

33. *Rental Brand Loyalty* (Livesy, 1973). Here BL is examined in the context of television rental agreements. Much as the exclusive purchase criterion, it is said to exist if the consumer continues the same rental agreement over time. For consumers terminating their contracts, only those switching to the rental of another brand are considered disloyal.

EVALUATION OF THE BEHAVIORAL INDICES

These definitions contain numerous and serious problems. First, and perhaps most basic, there has been virtually *no attempt to offer a logical-conceptual basis* for any of the operationalizations provided. The process of scientific inquiry requires that one first develop and state a clear concept of what one is going to measure before trying to develop measures adequate for assessing the phenomenon in question (see Chapter 4). As one consideration, is brand loyalty simply a form of repetitive behavior (perhaps somewhat like a reflex), or does it consist of something more? Having a precise concept in advance is central to the question of validity. Without such a concept how can we determine whether a measure is measuring "what it is supposed to measure"? None of the operational definitions described here seem to have been developed in such a manner. Several of the other problems noted later stem directly from this lack of a conceptual definition.

Second, *the criteria* used to distinguish between loyal and nonloyal consumers *are arbitrary and often appear unreasonable.* Consider the 50% criterion, or the three-in-a-row sequence criterion. What is the logical basis for saying that the individual who consistently devotes 40%

of his purchases to Brand *A* and then distributes the remaining 60% of purchases over any number of other brands is not loyal to Brand *A,* while one who devotes 50% of his purchases to Brand *A* is? And what about the individual whose 12 purchases produce a sequence as follows: *AABAACAADAAE,* and so on? Is he actually less loyal to Brand *A* than the individual whose sequence of 12 purchases looks like *AAA*BAC*AAA*DEA?

The arbitrary nature of some measures is cloaked in mathematics. Anderson's $(1 - \theta)m,$ for instance, assumes that purchasing not predicted by shelf space must necessarily be loyalty determined. Although little, if any, basis is provided in support of this assumption, this fact becomes lost, and the definition is all too readily accepted in the involved statistical estimation procedures that follow.

Third, in all likelihood, our *measures are overly simplistic.* Brand loyalty is most probably a complex, multifaceted phenomenon. Particularly if we do not begin with an overall concept of what it is (and what it is not), how do we know whether a given operational definition we are proposing is actually assessing each of its major facets? If BL is complex and multifaceted, adequate assessment may require that we use two or more different measurement approaches.

Fourth, our measurement efforts have not been *comprehensive* in yet another sense. From a philosophy of science perspective, attempts to study and understand a given phenomenon are generally enhanced if one also studies the opposite or negative case. With respect to BL this means studying the factors underlying *dis*loyalty. None of the behavioral definitions directly address this issue. They thereby forfeit this opportunity for acquiring valuable insight and understanding.

A fifth problem stems from not having a definition that specifies what the *unit of measurement* is or should be. This has two aspects. First, how many purchase occasions are necessary before it becomes meaningful to apply measures of repeat purchase? Second, is the measurement unit the individual or the group (e.g., a family)? If more than two people are involved, is it the decision-maker, the purchaser, or the user of the product—or some combination of the three—that should be the object of measurement? Many of the operational definitions provided are often derived from panel diary data collected from families who serve as the basic unit of measurement. In addition to the well-known problems of faulty recall and false claiming of purchases, such data do not permit us to determine whether the consistent purchasing of a brand represents loyalty on the part of the most influential individual in the family or the family itself or reflects a compromise among family members. Accordingly, when other data (such as personality scores) are collected from members of the family and then related to purchase data, the relationships found are meaningless if it cannot be demonstrated that the data collected are from the member(s) of the family who actually makes the decision about which brands should and should not be purchased.

A sixth problem with these definitions is that they are *based solely on overt purchase behavior*. As such, they represent the relatively static *outcome* of a dynamic decision process. However, none of the operational definitions described thus far seek to understand the factors underlying and leading up to brand-loyal purchasing; they make no attempt to explain the causative factors that determine how and especially why BL develops or is modified.

Seventh, the majority of these definitions *fail to accommodate multibrand loyalty*—the fact that consumers can be (and very often are) loyal to two or more brands in a product category. Consider, for example, the confirmed breakfast cereal eater who divides his purchases between 2 or 3 brands out of the more than 50 available to him in most supermarkets. It should be obvious that, unless a definition is capable of accommodating multibrand loyalty, it is necessarily incomplete.

Eighth, hardly any data exist to indicate the *relationships between and among the various measures*. Consider, for example, the conflicting conclusions that

might be reached from the following purchase sequences
made by four hypothetical consumers:

1. *AABAABAABA*
2. *BCDEFGHAAA*
3. *AABAACAAAD*
4. *AABAACAADA*

Person 1 is loyal according to the percent-of-purchase
definition (70% of his purchases being devoted to Brand
A) but is not loyal according to the three-in-a-row-sequence definition. In contrast Person 2 (who devoted
only 30% of his purchases to Brand *A*) is not loyal to
Brand *A* according to those percent-of-purchase definitions that employ a 50% cutoff criterion but is loyal to
Brand *A* according to the three-in-a-row-sequence definition. Person 1 is considered much more loyal to Brand *A*
than Person 3 according to Farley's N_{ar} (i.e., the number
of different brands purchased per unit time definition),
whereas Person 3 is considered loyal (and Person 1 not
loyal) according to the three-in-a-row-sequence definition. Persons 1 and 4 are equally loyal to Brand *A* according to the percent-of-purchase definitions; neither is loyal
to Brand *A* according to the three-in-a-row-sequence
definition; and Person 1 is more loyal than Person 4 according to Farley's N_{ar} definition. Persons 3 and 4 are
equally loyal according to both the N_{ar} and percent-of-
purchase definitions, while Person 4 is not loyal and
Person 3 is loyal according to the three-in-a-row-sequence definition. The fact that the three-in-a-row-sequence appeared more recently for Person 2 than for
Person 3 would also have been weighted more heavily in
some probability-of-purchase definitions than in others.
We have here considered only a few of the available
definitions. The problem takes on considerably greater
confusion as more and more different BL definitions are
applied to the same data base.

   Clearly, the same individual can be defined as loyal in
a study using one measure and nonloyal in a study using

a different measure of loyalty. Without having detailed knowledge of how these different measures interrelate, attempts to synthesize findings from different BL investigations into general principles and conclusions would seem to be a futile and meaningless task.

A ninth set of problems with regard to these operational definitions involves the consideration of *basic measurement desiderata,* namely, reliability, validity, and sensitivity. Of the measures just described, test-retest reliabilities have been provided for only three. These are the average length of brand runs (Number 12; $r = .810$, Massy, Frank, and Lodahl, 1968; $r = .918$, Olson and Jacoby, 1971), the three-in-a-row criterion (Number 10; $r = .746$, Olson and Jacoby, 1971), and the market-share concept (Number 2; $r = .690$, Massy, Frank, and Lodahl, 1968; $r = .863$, Olson and Jacoby, 1971).

Data regarding the predictive validity of these measures—particularly as they relate to predicting a *set* of future purchases rather than just the very next purchase—seem to be lacking, while data bearing on construct validity are available with respect to only three of these measures. Olson and Jacoby (1971) applied 12 different loyalty measures to the same group of subjects. A factor analysis of these data revealed that the market-share concept (Number 2), three-in-a-row criterion (Number 10), and average length of brand runs (Number 12) all loaded highly on a factor labeled "behavioral brand loyalty" that explained 27% of the variance.

Data are lacking on the sensitivity of a great many of these measures (i.e., their ability to distinguish between loyalty and nonloyalty and discriminate different degrees of loyalty). What information that can be found is largely negative. Consider Cunningham's market-share index (Number 2). Although this measure of BL is the one that appears most often in the literature, it seems to have serious drawbacks. It has been criticized by Massy, Frank, and Lodahl (1968) because of its tendency to conceal differences in the sequence of purchase. Day (1969) attacked it for including "spuriously" loyal consumers. Finally, there is the obvious problem that any cutoff point (e.g., Cunningham's 50% dividing line between loyal and nonloyal consumers) is highly arbitrary. Why not make the criterion 75%, as Lipstein did (Number 3), or 35% in a product category crowded with many brands?

Moreover, many of the criticisms directed at Cunningham's market-share index can be generalized to the other quantitatively more sophisticated measures. Consider Massy, Frank, and Lodahl's number of brand runs (Number 11) as an example. This measure fails to provide even an arbitrary cutoff point. It confounds store switching with brand switching and excludes much of the variance associated with proportion-of-purchase data. A high value on this measure could imply either a switching pattern due to real preference changes or "spurious" switching due to any one of a number of situational factors.

Intuitively, one might expect that the more sophisticated measures, such as Sheth's factor scores (Number 19), might pick up more information. And yet, data collected indicate that this may not be the case. "Correlations were computed between brand loyalty scores and the corresponding frequency of purchase . . . results indicate an almost perfect positive relationship . . . it was concluded that brand loyalty scores have negligible applied value" (Bodi, 1972). In short, very little new information appears to be gained with the application of the more elegant statistical techniques.

Although data are by no means plentiful, some general conclusions can be drawn with regard to the overall utility of the behavioral measures. First, test-retest reliabilities, although available on only a few indices, seem to be good. Second, while sensitivity of measurement varies greatly with the specific index used, the sensitivity of the behavioral measures seems, in general, to be poor. Finally, the vital data necessary for assessing predictive validity and, most especially,

construct validity are inadequate. These major problems—namely, (1) neglecting to offer a conceptual basis
for the operationalizations proposed; (2) providing arbitrary, simplistic, and sometimes unreasonable cutoff criteria; (3) failing to assess the complexity and richness of
BL; (4) neglecting to consider brand "disloyalty"; (5)
failing to specify the unit of measurement; (6) focusing on
the outcome of behavior and not developing definitions
that reach at the underlying causative factors; (7)
neglecting to accommodate for multibrand loyalty; (8)
failing to consider the interrelationships of the measure
being proposed with other measures of brand loyalty;
and (9) providing inadequate data regarding validity, reliability, and sensitivity—also apply to many of the
definitions about to be described. Hence, some of these
issues are not reiterated in each and every section.

ATTITUDINAL INDICES OF BRAND LOYALTY

Relative to the behavioral category, there are few (12, or
less than 25%) exclusively attitudinal measures of BL
(i.e., indices based solely on statements of preference or
intentions to behave, and not on actual purchase behavior). Many of these measures are of recent origin, and
their utility has only begun to be explored.

The rationale underlying most of the strictly attitudinal measures is that, while strictly behavioral
measures of BL may provide satisfactory prediction of
subsequent behavior, they are incapable of offering an
understanding of the factors underlying (i.e., causing) the
development and modification of BL. Attitudes are
considered to be the psychological construct most capable of providing such explanation.

Operational definitions based on attitudinal measures
are as follows:

34. *Brand Preference* (Guest, 1942). A consumer is defined
    as loyal to the brand he names in response to the ques-
    tion: Which brand do you prefer?

35. *Constancy of Preference* (Guest, 1955). Loyalty is said to exist if a similarity or constancy in favorable attitude toward brands can be found over a period of several years.

36. *Brand Name Loyalty* (Monroe and Guiltinan, 1975). Degrees of loyalty are assessed based on responses to the following seven-point rating scale item: "I make my purchase selection according to my favorite brand name, regardless of price."

37. *Distance between Acceptance and Rejection Regions* (Jacoby and Olson, 1970; Jacoby, 1971b). If brands are scaled along a continuum of brand preference, they divide themselves into general regions of acceptance (supposedly reflecting purchase tendencies), neutrality, and rejection. The greater the distance between accepted and rejected brands, the greater the degree of attitudinal BL. (Note: a wide variety of specific attitudinal scaling procedures can and have been used to generate such brand preference continua, including Fishbein—like value × expectancy procedures; see Olson and Jacoby, 1973).

38. *Distance between Acceptance and Neutrality Regions* (Jacoby and Olson, 1970; Jacoby, 1971b). As in definition 37, this involves a scaling of brands along a preference continuum. The greater the distance between accepted and neutral brands, the greater the degree of attitudinal brand loyalty.

39. *Relative Range of Region* (Jacoby and Olson, 1970; Jacoby, 1971b). Instead of using the distance between regions, one can use the range encompassed by a region (i.e., the distance between the highest and lowest brand scale values within that region) and express it as a percentage of the total range of scale values. The greater the span of the rejection region and the shorter the span of the acceptance region (i.e., R/A, where R and A represent the percentage of total brands found in the rejection and acceptance regions, respectively), the greater the degree of BL.

40. *Number (or Proportion) of Brands in the Acceptance Region* (Jacoby and Olson, 1970; Jacoby, 1971b). As the actual number of brands in the acceptance region increases, the extent of BL displayed toward more than one brand (i.e., multibrand loyalty) is expected to increase and the degree of unibrand loyalty to decrease.

41. *Number (or Proportion) of Brands in the Rejection Region* (Jacoby and Olson, 1970; Jacoby, 1971b). As the number of brands in the rejection region increases (and thereby reflects the fact that the consumer has devoted a certain amount of time and effort to cognitively considering and evaluating the brands in the product category), the extent of loyalty to any brands in the acceptance region is expected to increase.

42. *Modified Measure of Attitudinal Regions* (Bennett and Kassarjian, 1972). Here BL is said to equal R/A $(1.0 - NC)$, where R, A, and NC stand for the percentage of total brands found in the rejection, acceptance, and noncommitment regions, respectively.

43. *Cognitive Loyalty* (Jarvis and Wilcox, 1976). Loyalty is defined as the ratio of rejected brands to accepted brands weighted by an index of brand awareness. The following equation is given:

$$\text{cognitive loyalty} = (RR/AR) \times (1 - [BA - (RR + AR)]/BA)$$

where RR = the number of brands in the rejection region
AR = the number of brands in the acceptance region
BA = the number of brands of which the consumer is aware

44. *Psychographic Scaling* (Reynolds, Darden, and Martin, 1974). Store loyalty is measured by a four-item scaling procedure. The items are embedded in a questionnaire containing 144 psychographic statements. Responses are collected by use of a six-point scale, and the data for the

four items are summated to give a total score. These
items are:

1. I do most of my shopping in the same stores
    I have always shopped in.
2. Once I get used to where things are in a supermarket,
    I hate to change stores.
3. I like things the old, established way.
4. Once I have made a choice of which store to buy
    clothes in, I am likely to shop there without trying
    other stores.

45. *Intent-to-Purchase Measure* (Jacoby, Jones, and
    Chestnut, in preparation). By use of Juster's (1966) 11-
    point "probability-of-purchase" scale, brands within a
    specific product class are distributed along an intent-to-
    purchase continuum. Zones of acceptance and rejection
    can be defined as with measures 37–43. Certain other
    parameters relating to the nature of the distribution of
    brands (e.g., breaks within the distribution to form
    regions, number of brands in each region, number of
    probability intervals encompassed by each region) can be
    examined with regard to BL.

EVALUATION OF ATTITUDINAL INDICES

Many of the attitudinal-operational definitions would
seem to make rather fine interval-like distinctions
between degrees of BL. By means of scaling techniques
such as the Bradley, Terry, and Luce model, several of
the measures developed by Jacoby and his colleagues,
for instance, can work with exact distances between
scale values. Whether or not these distances are actual
representations of attitudinal distinctions in the mind of
the consumer is, however, a question yet to be
answered. As suggested earlier in the context of Sheth's
factor scores, the more sophisticated techniques often

lend themselves to artifact, as well as to increased sensitivity.

Measures based on a scaling of regions of neutrality and rejection in addition to regions of acceptance do, however, offer specific advantages. These measures are predicated on the assumption that one must study reactions to all brands in a product class—rejected as well as accepted—to understand loyalty to any one specific brand adequately. The distance between the acceptance and the rejection regions, for example, is not a function of dissimilarity between the least and the most preferred brand but a measurement of the distance between two sets of related brands (i.e., those being "accepted" and those being "rejected" by the consumer). This multi-brand orientation greatly increases the amount of information in the scaling by placing a given brand in the context of its competition.

Test-retest reliabilities are available on three of the attitudinal measures. Olson and Jacoby (1971), using the same questionnaire administered three weeks apart to a group of toothpaste purchasers, provide coefficients for the constancy of preference over time (Number 35; $r = .798$), as well as for preliminary and very crude measures of the number of brands in the acceptance region (Number 40; $r = .587$) and of the number of brands in the rejection region (Number 41; $r = .399$). In a later study using Sherif's "ordered alternatives" sorting procedure for scaling accepted and rejected brands, Jacoby, Olson, and Szybillo (1971) found improved coefficients (ranging from .5 to .6) for both "number of brands" measures (i.e., Numbers 40 and 41). These three indices have also been found to load highly on "multiple brand loyalty" and "attitudinal brand loyalty" factors. Together, these 2 factors explained 32% of the variance in a factor analysis of 12 BL measures administered concurrently to the same group of subjects (see Olson and Jacoby, 1971).

Data collected on the validity of the attitudinal measures have been unencouraging. Jacoby, Olson, and

Szybillo (1971) compared several different scaling procedures for generating the "number of brands" measures in terms of the Campbell and Fiske (1959) multitrait, multimethod matrix and, in general, obtained low positive correlations (i.e., "poor" results). Although they supported the notion that the attitudinal measures have good discriminant validity with respect to behavioral indices (i.e., they explained a different portion of the variance associated with BL), their study failed to show acceptable levels of convergent validity. The attitudinal measures used in that investigation did not relate (significantly) as hypothesized with other constructs, such as stated brand commitment, perceived product importance, or perceived risk.

In summary, therefore, it would appear that attitudinal measures of BL developed thus far have their limitations. Although on the face of it they appear to provide greater sensitivity, no empirical support has been provided to warrant such a conclusion. Their test-retest reliabilities seem adequate but are available for only 3 of the 12 measures. Finally, although predictive of a unique portion of the variance associated with BL, they have not related as hypothesized with other variables. Some of these problems (especially that of convergent validity) may, however, be resolved by new techniques being used for scaling attitudinal regions (e.g., Number 45).

COMPOSITE INDICES OF BRAND LOYALTY

The composite measures of BL involve an integration of behavioral and attitudinal approaches. Most of these measures are of more recent origin, which partially explains why there are relatively few of these described in the published literature.

46. *Brand Insistence* (Copeland, 1923). This measure combines the behavioral index of exclusive purchase with an

out-of-stock decision that another brand would be purchased only in the case of an emergency.

47. *Price until Switching* (Pessemier, 1959). The respondent's (MPB) is determined and then, over a set of 10 or 15 purchase trials during which the prices of all other brands remain as they were, the price of the MPB is raised in constant increments (e.g., 1¢ per trial) until the point at which the consumer either switches to another brand or the designated trial series is completed. The index of BL is the number of trials (i.e., price increases) necessary to induce switching. Increasing the price of the MPB is not, however, the only way that this measure can be set up. Pessemier (and Jacoby and Kyner, 1973) decreased the prices of all other brands while leaving the price of the MPB constant. Generally, results appear similar across such alternate manipulations. Tucker (1964) and McConnell (1968a) used other variants of this approach.

48. *Stated Brand Commitment* (Cunningham, 1967). Previous purchase behavior is assessed by first asking the consumer if there is any one brand of the product in question that he buys consistently. If his answer is "yes," he is then asked to imagine that he has gone to purchase this product and, while in the first retail outlet, has found that his favorite brand is out of stock. Under these circumstances, would he: (1) go to another store, (2) wait to purchase his favorite brand until another shopping trip, or (3) buy an alternate brand at that point in time? The loyal consumer is operationally defined as one who asserts (in response to Question 1) that he usually buys one particular brand of the product and (in response to Question 2), upon finding this brand out of stock, says he would either proceed to another store to locate this brand or wait until another shopping trip and look for it then.

49. L_i (Day, 1969). Day's loyalty index is defined as the ratio of the proportion of purchases devoted to Brand i to the initial attitude toward Brand i ($L_i = P(B_i)/A_i$).

50. *Bayesian Loyalty Measure* (Lutz and Winn, 1975). This measure is basically quite comparable to L_i divided by

the variance. The loyalty of Consumer i to Brand j is defined as follows:

$$BLM_{ij} = Z_{AX_{ij}} \Big/ (Z_{AS_{ij}} + C_{A_j}) + Z_{BX_{ij}} \Big/ (Z_{BS_{ij}} + C_{B_j})$$

where $Z_{AX_{ij}}$ = a standardized mean attitude score
Z_{AS_j} = the standardized variance of the attitude score
C_{A_j} = an arbitrary constant added to make all standardized variance scores positive
$Z_{BX_{ij}}$ = a weighted mean of Consumer i's purchase behavior. Specifically, it is the mean purchasing of Brand j weighted by a factor corrected for the amount of purchasing within the time period being examined. This is then standardized
$Z_{BS_{ij}}$ = the standardized variance of the behavioral score
C_{B_j} = an arbitrary constant added to make all standardized variance scores positive.

51. *Information Search* (Newman and Werbel, 1973). This measure is primarily directed toward measuring BL with respect to durable goods. Loyalty scores range from 10 to 50 (higher scores having greater BL) and are assigned on the basis of verbal reports to a series of questions regarding prepurchase information search. The questioning procedure and scoring system can be diagramed as in Figure 3.1.

52. *Package Search* (Towle and Martin, 1976). A more limited form of information search measure (confining attention to search behavior devoted to manufacturer's name), this reflects an attitudinal predisposition toward the manufacturer's name. Loyal consumers are defined as those agreeing with the statement: "I always look for the name of the manufacturer on the package." Responses are collected on a five-point Likert scaling using the following anchors: agree a lot, agree a little, not sure, disagree a little, and disagree a lot.

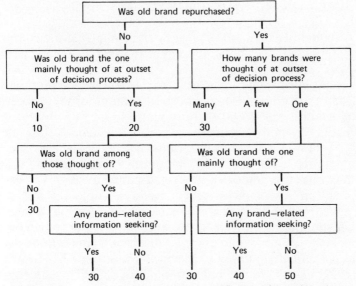

Figure 3.1 The "information search" definition of brand loyalty

53. *Composite Store Loyalty* (Bellenger, Steinberg, and Stanton, 1976). A multivariate measure of store loyalty is computed according to the following three steps:

1. A subjective estimate of the percent of shopping devoted to a given store is obtained.
2. A number of stores are then ranked on the following criteria: product line, distance and time involved in shopping, attitude of store personnel, climate or atmosphere of store, and availability of parking. Ranks for a given store are reversed and used to weight the percent obtained in Step 1.
3. Finally, consumers are asked to respond to the statement: "I shop at (name of store) when I need an item I think they carry." A five-point scaling is used with the anchors of strongly agree, agree, neutral, disagree, and strongly disagree. These are then scored from strongly agree (5) to strongly disagree (1) and used to weight the result of Step 2.

EVALUATION OF THE COMPOSITE INDICES

Although it is not yet clear how the composite measures compare with the behavioral or attitudinal measures, two points speak in their favor. First, as Day (1969) has shown, attitudinal measures may be used to screen out "spuriously loyal" consumers from an otherwise purely behavioral index and thereby increase the sensitivity of that behavioral measure.

Second, many of the composite methods are "behavioroid". Aronson and Carlsmith (1968) contend that, in contrast to standard paper-and-pencil measures, "behavioroid" measures reflect greater subject involvement. Rather than simply check a response blank on a questionnaire, the subject is required actually to behave in some fashion while engaged in either a simulation or a hypothetical shopping situation. Aronson and Carlsmith (1968) use the term "behavior*oid*" to describe such surrogates for real-world behavior*al* measures. By combining some elements of both behavior and attitude and by increasing subject involvement in the experimental task, such composite behavioroid measures have the potential for greater sensitivity.

Some of the measures have, however, introduced certain confounding factors into their definition. Cunningham's stated-brand-commitment measure (Number 48), for example, combines measurement of store loyalty with assessment of BL. The measure also allows for the collection of ambiguous data. For instance, how do we classify the consumer who states no consistent purchasing tendencies toward a single brand but who, in response to the second question, states that he would wait until a later shopping trip if a particular brand were out of stock?

Test-retest reliabilities are available on only two of the composite measures. These are the price-until-switching index (Number 47; $r = .819$) and the stated-brand-commitment index (Number 48; $r = .770$; see Olson and Jacoby, 1971). Both measures load simultaneously on the "behavioral" and "attitudinal" components of the Olson and Jacoby (1971) factor solution.

This double loading (i.e., the explanation of variance associated with attitude as well as with behavior) would lead one to believe that such measures might have a greater construct validity (cf. Lutz and Winn, 1975). When loyalty is restricted to either behavior or attitude alone, it seems incomplete: witness the independence of these factors in the Olson and Jacoby (1971) principal components analysis. Construct validity tends to be improved by the simple fact that composite operational definitions include more of the construct (i.e., the reality of both behavioral and attitudinal aspects of BL). Pessemier, for example, first established loyalty to an MPB and then strained that loyalty by altering prices. It was the strength of the consumer's attitude toward the MPB that determined how long he would put up with such changes.

In summary, although certain measurement problems are apparent in the composite definitions, the approach seems valuable. Sensitivity seems to be enhanced, available test-retest reliabilities are high, and construct validity appears improved. The basic argument against such measures is that, thus far, they typically use laboratory experimentation for assessing the behavioral component. Such a restriction may well be undesirable in the applied context of marketing research.

CHAOS IN RESEARCHLAND:
THE SORRY STATUS OF
BRAND LOYALTY MEASUREMENT

Despite the hundreds of published studies now available on BL, the data necessary for evaluating the adequacy of the available indices are almost nowhere to be found. Almost every single one of these investigations has been concerned with attempting to identify *relationships* between indices of BL and other variables and has ignored the logically prior issue of ensuring that the *indices* themselves satisfied basic measurement criteria, most particularly, the criterion of validity.* Until and unless we can be assured that the measure employed in a given study is a valid indicant of BL, we cannot and should not accept the purported "findings" of that investigation as valid. But just what is BL? This pivotal question provides the focus for much of the remainder of this monograph.

A basic objective the authors had at the outset was to identify a limited set of "good" BL measures that could then be used in subsequent research activities. To do so requires that we first specify "good in terms of what?" That is, what criteria should be used in assessing the adequacy of a BL measure? A list of such criteria, including the three most fundamental and standard measurement criteria (i.e., validity, reliability, and sensitivity), as well as other desiderata, follows.

1. *Validity.* The issue of validity takes into consideration numerous subquestions.
    a. Does the measure make sense in terms of how BL is conceptually defined? That is, does it seem to be directed to measuring what it is supposed to be measuring?
    b. Relatedly, does the measure encompass all aspects of BL? (A prior question that must be answered is: Just what are the various aspects of BL?) For example, does the measure accommodate multibrand loyalty, or is it only a unibrand measure?
    c. Does the measure relate as predicted to other measures of BL, as well as to other variables (e.g., perceived risk, perceived quality differences, being a working vs. nonworking wife)?

*Chapter 4 represents an elaboration of the issues, problems, and necessary directions suggested by this sentence.

2. *Reliability*. Does the measure yield consistent results, given that the same circumstances prevail at the different points in time at which measurements are taken?
3. *Sensitivity*. Is the measure capable of adequately discriminating between the presence or absence (and, if present, among different degrees) of the phenomenon (i.e., can it distinguish different intensities of loyalty)?
4. Does the measure focus only on the outcome of behavior, or does it also incorporate elements designed to assess the decision process dynamics underlying and determining BL?
5. How do subjects respond to the measure? Is it "reactive"? That is, does it introduce artifacts by causing consumers to behave or respond in manners in which they would not otherwise behave or respond?
6. How closely do the circumstances of measurement approximate real-world conditions?
7. What are the costs and ease of both administration and scoring?

In reviewing the available literature, it quickly became obvious that hardly any data have been provided for assessing the adequacy of any of the proposed BL measures. Table 3.1 provides a summary of what is available that bears on the prerequisite measurement considerations of validity, reliability, and sensitivity of the 53 operational measures discussed above. It can easily be seen from this table that the data necessary for assessing measurement adequacy have *never* been provided for most of the indices. Investigators have either ignored these issues or simply assumed that the measures they were using possessed adequate validity, reliability, and sensitivity. Their concern, instead, was with identifying relationships between the purported "measure" of BL they were using and measures of other variables (see Figure 4.1 in Chapter 4). In other words, the necessary developmental spadework that normally and logically precedes the use of a measure is almost totally missing from the literature on BL.

Table 3.1 AVAILABLE DATA BEARING ON THE SENSITIVITY, RELIABILITY, AND VALIDITY OF THE 53 BL MEASURES.

BL Measure	Sensitivity	Reliability	Validity
1. Exclusive purchase	Limited	?	?
2. Market-share concept	Poor (Day, 1969)	$r = .86$ (Olson & Jacoby, 1971)	?
3. Hard-core criterion	?	?	?
4. Two-thirds criterion	?	?	?
5. Dual brand loyalty	?	?	?
6. Triple brand loyalty	?	?	?
7. FRA	?	?	?
8. Divided loyalty	?	?	?
9. Unstable loyalty	?	?	?
10. Three-in-a-row criterion	?	$r = .75$ (Olson & Jacoby, 1971)	?
11. Number of brand runs	?	?	Confounds store with brand switching
12. Average length of brand runs	?	$r = .92$ (Olson & Jacoby, 1971) $r = .81$ (Massy, Frank, & Lodahl, 1968)	Confounds store with brand switching
13. First-order (Markov) probability of repurchase	?	?	?
14. Average staying time	?	?	?
15. Repeat purchase probability	?	?	?
16. Return purchase probability	?	?	?
17. $P(B_t|B_{t_{n-1}}) - P(B_t)$	?	?	Longitudinal measure
18. The shopping matrix	?	?	?
19. Sheth factor scores	?	?	No improvement on market share (Bodi, 1972)
20. Massy, Frank, & Lodahl factor scores	?	?	?

BL Measure	Sensitivity	Reliability	Validity
21. Loyalty index	?	?	?
22. Θ (entropy measure)	?	?	?
23. Lost-gained ratio	?	?	Arbitrary (Cunningham, 1956)
24. N_m	?	?	?
25. S_m	?	?	?
26. N_{ar}	?	?	?
27. S_{ar}	?	?	?
28. $(1 - \Theta)m$	?	?	?
29. Estimate by elimination	?	?	?
30. Private brand loyalty	?	?	?
31. New resident loyalty	?	?	?
32. Dealer agency loyalty	?	?	?
33. Rental brand loyalty	?	?	?
34. Brand preference	?	?	?
35. Constancy of preference	?	$r = .80$ (Olson & Jacoby, 1971)	?
36. Brand name loyalty	?	?	?
37. Distance between acceptance and rejection regions	?	?	In doubt (Jacoby, Olson, & Szybillo, 1971)
38. Distance between acceptance and neutrality regions	?	?	In doubt (Jacoby, Olson & Szybillo, 1971)
39. Relative range of region	?	?	In doubt (Jacoby, Olson, & Szybillo, 1971)
40. Number of brands in the acceptance region	?	$r = .59$ (Olson & Jacoby, 1971) $r = .5$ to $.6$ (Jacoby, Olson, & Szybillo, 1971)	In doubt (Jacoby, Olson, & Szybillo, 1971)

Table 3.1 (continued)

BL Measure	Sensitivity	Reliability	Validity
41. Number of brands in the rejection region	?	$r = .40$ (Olson & Jacoby, 1971)	In doubt (Jacoby, Olson, & Szybillo, 1971)
		$r = .5$ to $.6$ (Jacoby, Olson, & Szybillo, 1971)	
42. Bennett and Kassarjian's measure of attitudinal regions	?	?	?
43. Cognitive loyalty	?	?	?
44. Psychographic scaling	?	?	Factor analysis supports (Reynolds, Darden, & Martin, 1974)
45. Intent to purchase measure	?	?	?
46. Brand insistence	?	?	?
47. Price-until-switching	?	$r = .82$ (Olson & Jacoby, 1971)	?
48. Stated brand commitment	?	$r = .77$ (Olson & Jacoby, 1971)	Confounds store and brand loyalty
49. L_i	Improvement on market share (Day, 1969)	?	?
50. Bayesian loyalty measure	?	?	Tentative support (Lutz & Winn, 1975)
51. Information search	?	?	?
52. Package search	?	?	?
53. Composite store loyalty	?	?	?

Only two published studies appear to exist that administered three or more BL measures concurrently to the same group of subjects and thereby permitted an examination of how these measures interrelated (see Massy, Frank, and Lodahl, 1968; Olson and Jacoby, 1971). Data from one of these studies have recently been reanalyzed (see Mitchell and Olson, 1975) by use of a different statistical approach. Only one published study seems to exist (see Olson and Jacoby, 1971) that measured the test-retest reliability of a set of BL measures (although some unpublished work has also addressed this issue; see Jacoby, Olson, and Szybillo, 1971). Not many of us would feel comfortable using a thermometer to measure our body temperature if, with no actual change in our body temperature, the thermometer gave us readings of 97.0°, 100.6°, 98.6°, and 102.0° within the space of one 15-minute period. Yet we persistently employ BL indices of unknown reliability to study consumer purchase decisions and behavior and sometimes develop nationwide promotional strategies based on data collected with such indices.

In contrast to shoehorning data to fit preconceived notions regarding BL components (see Burford, Enis, and Paul, 1971; Day, 1969), only one published (Olson and Jacoby, 1971) and one unpublished (Rice, 1962) study sought to arrive at a description of the various facets or components of BL based on an empirical analysis of data obtained. The Olson and Jacoby (1971) analysis (since replicated in other unpublished investigations conducted by the same authors that used different subjects and products) suggests that BL has at least the following four components: behavioral, attitudinal, multibrand loyalty, and a small (in terms of the amount of variance explained) general-brand loyalty component (i.e., being brand loyal across a variety of different products). No comprehensive measure has yet been provided in the published literature that encompasses all four of these components. Like intelligence and personality, BL is a complex phenomenon. The reader is urged to ask himself how comfortable and satisfied he would be to have either his intelligence or personality "definitively assessed" on the basis of his response to a single item. Yet this is essentially the same kind of unreasonable demand we make of our BL measures.

Finally, where is any BL research that directly addresses the issue of sensitivity? Assume that our new thermometer was both valid and reliable. How useful would it be if it used scale points that could discriminate only between temperature differences greater than 5° Fahrenheit, so that it showed no difference between actual temperatures of 99° and 103°?

Thus, despite our desire to identify one or a few "good" measures of BL for use in future research, there are insufficient and inadequate data available on which to base such judgments. Considerable developmental work, particularly involving cross-index comparisons (very much like Axelrod's [1968] effort with respect to advertising effectiveness measures), is needed before one can reasonably and justifiably designate any BL measure(s) as being any better or worse than the others.

Stated somewhat differently, most published BL research is no more sophisticated (or valid) than having a "researcher" first arbitrarily, without any empirical justification, assert that the number of pebbles a person can count in a 10-minute period is an indicant of that person's intelligence; next, conduct a study and find that people who can count many pebbles in 10 minutes also tend to eat more; and, finally, conclude from this: people with high intelligence tend to eat more. Such a "researcher" would become the laughing stock of the research community. Unfortunately, this is the sorry state of most BL research today. In only a very few instances—namely, where a particular finding appears with relative consistency across several studies employing different indices—is it *perhaps* justifiable to cite findings as being relatively well established and likely to hold up under more rigorous empirical scrutiny.

In sum, we see BL measurement in chaos and characterized by many problems. Although we have focused in this section on the basic measurement issues of validity, reliability, and sensitivity, the preceding sections noted additional problems, some of which are directly related to the issue of validity raised above. In general, these include: (1) failure to provide conceptual bases for the operationalization(s) proposed; (2) arbitrary and often unreasonable cutoff criteria; (3) failure to move away from simplistic formulations to formulations that address the complexity and richness of BL, that is, that assess its different facets; (4) failure to accommodate for the fact that consumers can be and often are loyal to a subset of brands within a product category, that is, are multibrand loyal; (5) focusing on the relatively static outcome of behavior without giving due consideration to the underlying and most likely dynamic causative factors; (6) failure to consider the phenomenon in terms of its broader context, namely, loyalty-disloyalty; (7) having internally inconsistent and/or ambiguous elements, for example, as with the confusion between brand and store loyalty; (8) failure to specify the appropriate unit for measurement, that is, the purchaser, user, and/or decision-maker; and (9) failure to consider the interrelationship of the measure being proposed with other purported measures of BL.

Does this mean that BL is a blind alley and that devoting time, money, and effort to this research would be an unwise investment of resources for marketing managers? Definitely not! Sound BL research has enormous potential for contributing to our understanding of consumer behavior and assisting decision-makers to reach applied marketing objectives. A basic requirement for realizing this potential is that investigators approach the subject with their research priorities in correct order. In brief, what is needed is a concentrated effort that focuses on the development and validation of BL measures. It is only *after* such appropriate measures have been developed that attempts to identify specific relationships between BL and other variables can be meaningfully undertaken.

The next chapter outlines the steps necessary for developing satisfactory and valid measures of BL. Given the availability of satisfactory indices, the final chapter outlines how we can proceed to conduct research having both applied and basic utility.

A MANAGER'S GUIDE TO

Conceptual Definitions, Theory,

AND

Construct Validation

Quite clearly, despite several hundred published articles on the subject, it is not yet possible to point to one or a select few indices and, with any degree of confidence or justification, say: "These are the satisfactory, good, appropriate, or valid measures of brand loyalty." Consideration of the brand loyalty (BL) literature suggests that a basic reason behind this lack of progress is

the absence of explicit and agreed-upon conceptual
definitions to serve as the bases on which to develop indices of BL and guide research. The significance of this
problem cannot be overemphasized; indeed, it is fundamental and crucial. This chapter is addressed to distinguishing between conceptual and operational definitions,
describing the problems underlying the strictly operational definitions, indicating why conceptual definitions
of BL are so necessary, providing one such definition,
and outlining the approach used in attempting to assess
the validity of a conceptual definition.

CONCEPTUAL AND
OPERATIONAL DEFINITIONS

What is BL? We might just as well ask what friendship,
intelligence, opinion leadership, or personality is. Reply-
ing that "intelligence is what intelligence tests measure"
is unsatisfactory; it begs the question. Seemingly less
abstract phenomena provide similar difficulty. As examples, what is price? distance? size? All of us have some
general idea of what these words mean in everyday
speech. But as noted below, even in this context there is
considerable ambiguity. Is this adequate for scientific
(whether basic or applied) research? Definitely not—and
neither is it for managerial decision-making. Effective decision-making requires precision in language.
Words that convey meaning imprecisely or ambiguously
can result in all forms of mayhem, corporate and
otherwise. Precision in meaning is a prerequisite for both
good science and good management.

"How large is your company?" the insurance pros-
pect asked of the agent. Does the salesperson reply in
terms of the number of states in which this company
maintains a sales operation, the total number of people in
this company's sales force, the total number of em-
ployees (both in sales and otherwise), the amount of in-

surance the company has in force, its assets-to-liabilities ratio, and so forth?

And what about the researcher trying to determine whether and where to erect a new shopping center? He begins by asking a sample of people in the target area what they want most in a shopping mall and learns that "convenience" is highly regarded. He is not, however, quite sure what this means, since, in response to further probing, he learns that the same word means many things to many people (including enough places to park one's car, close physical proximity of the shopping center to other places that the individual frequents, and the distance from the individual's home). The researcher decides to explore the issue of "distance" further. However, the question "How far away is the XYZ shopping center?" produced the following five replies from five different people: "two subway stops; three traffic lights; ten minutes; three miles; across the street from the Standard station." Obviously, even commonly used concepts such as "size" and "distance" can take many specific expressions.

But surely, everyone knows what "price" is. After all, most of us purchase things daily in exchange for which we present the seller with that societally recognized token of our esteem called money. In actuality, price is also a very nebulous concept (see Jacoby and Olson, 1977). Is it equivalent to or different from "cost"? Does it include only the "ticket price" or also the tax and finance charges? What about the expenditure of time in the acquisition of product? Since time and effort can be translated into monetary value, some economists (Becker, 1965; Linder, 1970) might consider these factors to constitute part of price. In addition, actual monetary costs involved in travel, postpurchase usage (such as for installation or maintenance), and in disposing of the product once it has outlived its usefulness might all be considered part of price. A recent MIT report noted that the total financial life-cycle costs involved in owning a refrigerator consisted of 36% devoted

to the initial acquisition, 6% to service, and 58% to
electrical power (MIT, 1974). Finally, in their efforts to
develop a suitable approach for disclosing life insurance
cost information to the consumer, the Federal Trade
Commission includes in its concept of cost the difference
between the amount of money the individual would
receive from the policy dividends and the amount of
interest he would have received if he had placed the cash
equivalent into a savings account.

In raising these issues, we are trying to illustrate the
two basic types of definitions, conceptual and operational. *Conceptual definitions* are abstractions. They
represent attempts to encompass in some symbolic form
(usually language) the essence of what we mean when we
speak about a particular item, phenomenon, or event. In
contrast, defining a concept in terms of the instrument or
processes used to measure that concept is called "operationalism" and such definitions are termed *operational
definitions*. Thus operational definitions of BL are
basically detailed descriptions of the procedures used to
measure loyalty. For example: collect panel data for one
year from a given sample of respondents; for any given
respondent, tabulate the number of times that a
particular product (e.g., breakfast cereal) was
purchased; then tally the number of times each brand in
this product category was purchased; finally, label as BL
any instance in which one of the competing brands is
purchased 51% or more of the time during this period.

There may be a variety of different ways to give empirical form to (i.e., measure) a given concept. In operationalizing "hunger," psychologists have: (1) asked
people to respond to questionnaire items regarding their
degree of perceived hunger; (2) deprived different individuals of food for different amounts of time so as supposedly to create more hunger in some than in others
(e.g., people deprived for 16 hours must surely be more
hungry than those deprived for only 2 hours); (3)
measured the amount of food consumed from a standard
portion given to each subject (e.g., 2 pounds of
spaghetti), under the assumption that the more one

consumes (perhaps adjusted by one's body weight, metabolism, etc.), the hungrier one is; and (4) measured the amount of adversity the organism (often rats in shock boxes) will go through to obtain food. As we have observed, many ways have also been proposed to measure BL.

Defining a phenomenon is further complicated by researchers' often disagreeing among themselves about what constitutes the common essence of the phenomenon under question. Thus, not only may a single conceptual definition give rise to a variety of operational definitions, but also there may be numerous conceptual definitions. Given that each investigator makes his conceptual definition explicit (in terms of clearly articulated and precisely defined propositions), specific points of agreement and disagreement can be identified. The former may be assumed to represent the essential core (i.e., agreed-upon or "shared" meaning) of the concept, while the latter may be amenable to empirical resolution.

Assuming that we have clearly articulated and precisely defined conceptual and operational definitions, which should we use? The answer is both. Conceptual definitions alone yield no data (Selltiz et al., 1960, p. 42), and operational definitions cannot exist without at least some germ of a conceptual definition. The critical question is, not which to use, but in what sequence.

PROBLEMS WITH PURELY OPERATIONAL DEFINITIONS

Treatises on science* universally agree that, before we can adequately measure a phenomenon, object, or event, we must have some idea of what it is we are trying to

---

*We use the term *science* in its traditional generic sense as referring to the interplay between ideas (concepts, theories, models) and research conducted to confirm or disconfirm these ideas. In this regard, scientific research may be either basic or applied.

measure (e.g., Massaro, 1975, p. 23; Plutchik, 1968, p. 45; Selltiz et al., 1960, pp. 146–147.) "The choice of operations should depend on the result of a conceptual analysis of the essential features of a construct" (Cook and Campbell, 1976, p. 241). "The concept always comes first, and then certain procedures (or operations) are selected from a larger possible number and used as *indicators* of the concept" (Plutchik, 1968, p. 49). The starting point is thus the *concept*.

Once developed on the basis of some concept, scientific measures rarely remain static and unchanged over time. "Science develops its measuring tools, typically, by a series of successive approximations in which the concept gradually achieves greater precision . . ." (Plutchik, 1968, p. 45). As research findings are interrelated and interpreted, they feed back to produce refinements and greater precision in our ability to specify the concept. In turn, as a result, the approaches to measure the concept are modified accordingly. This is true in the physical sciences, becoming true in the social sciences, and should be true if management is ever to become a true science.

Consideration of the literature reveals that this cyclical process of refinement in measurement has failed to surface in the published work on BL. Once proposed, our measures of BL seem to take on an almost inviolate existence all their own. They are rarely, if ever, critically examined or questioned. It is not hard to see why. In general, investigators have ignored the necessity of separating the concept being measured from the measurement procedure or instrument being used. As examples, instead of its being viewed as an *indicator of* BL, investigators typically consider devoting 51% of one's purchases to Brand X *to be* BL. Instead of considering six purchases of Brand X in a row to be an *indicator* of loyalty, investigators consider this *to be* BL itself. Thus the concept under investigation (namely, BL) has no identity separate from the instruments or procedures being used to measure it. Researchers of BL have relied on operational definitions and all but completely disregarded the necessity for specifying their conceptual definitions.

Although popular in the social sciences during the first half of this century, primarily because of its apparent objectivity (see *Psychology Review,* 1945), the more advanced sciences have long ago discarded the approach of defining a phenomenon *strictly* in terms of the operations used to measure it. Operational definitions were found to have numerous significant problems. Perhaps most important, they are "a very inadequate way of defining any concept because (they) can produce results which are obviously meaningless" (Plutchik, 1968, p. 44). For example, one could operationally define BL in terms of the amount of water a person could drink in 10 minutes: the greater the amount of water a person can drink during this period, the greater is his or her BL. We could then be exceedingly precise in specifying how to measure water consumption during a standard 10-minute period—even to the point of having our research subjects fast for 12 hours before coming to our laboratory, providing them with a standard beaker containing 1240 cc of water having a specified mineral content, timing the 10-minute period to the millisecond, precisely measuring the water actually consumed by each respondent during this period, and collecting retest reliability estimates under the same conditions 10 days later. Yet none of this precision or objectivity is likely to mean very much—at least in terms of BL. "Operationism provides no basis for distinguishing between meaningful and meaningless concepts" (Plutchik, 1968, p. 45).

A second problem with operational definitions is that, by asserting that "our procedures measure BL and BL is what our procedures measure," all criticism of the procedures and definitions is automatically excluded. "To be able to judge the relative value of measurements or of operations requires criteria beyond the operations themselves. If a concept is nothing but an operation, how can we talk about being mistaken or about making errors?'' (Plutchik, 1968, p. 47). In other words, operationalism does not permit the evaluation of any operational measure nor does it provide any basis for selecting which is the "better" measure, given that we have two or more measures. In point of fact, often "some inconsequential aspects are chosen [to represent a concept] because of their ready observability and measurability" (Guilford, 1956, p. 463).

This relates directly to another problem stemming from science's being basically a highly social enterprise (see Nunnally, 1967; Selltiz et al., 1960).

> It is not consistent with science for a particular investigator to simply say that his method of measuring something provides an operational definition. If this were done, then each investigator might have his own private operational definition of each concept and communication between researchers would completely break down. In practice, each scientist's procedures for measuring concepts must relate in some reasonable way to the work of other investigators as well as to the history of that idea (Plutchik, 1968, p. 49).

It is a rare occasion, indeed, when a BL researcher relates his measure to measures used by others, and it is even rarer for the same investigator to apply two or more different measures of BL in the same study to the same sample.

A fourth problem concerns errors of both commission and omission. Without an explicit conceptual definition to serve a guiding function, it is easy to see how operational definitions often generate problems both by including inconsequential or irrelevant elements while at the same time neglecting important aspects of the phenomenon under consideration.

Fifth, if the concept being measured is indeed synonymous with the measurement procedures or instrument being used, then even minute changes in method must necessarily produce new concepts. One consequence of such a proliferation of definitions would be confusion and an inability to communicate precisely regarding the concept. "When this occurs, generalizations involving the construct [i.e., concept] are impossible to make since there is really no single construct under investigation but, instead, a multitude of constructs" (Bohrnstedt, 1970, pp. 94–95).

Finally, strict adherence to operationalism "means that both the results of an [investigation] and the conclusions the investigators derive from it can never transcend the methodology employed" (Chaplin and Krawiec, 1960, p. 4). Thus our ability to generalize is severely abridged.

Unfortunately, these problems are all amply reflected in the BL literature. Measures of BL that appear to be basically meaningless continue to be developed and employed. Criteria for assessing the adequacy of any given operational definition are nowhere to be found. These definitions are constructed and used more at the whim of the investigator rather than because they have been demonstrated in fact to be better indicants of what he wishes to measure. As is quite clearly indicated in the preceding chapter, we have a proliferation of definitions. Almost all the ones developed thus far are still in use today, and efforts to identify and weed out the poorer measures are virtually nonexistent. The ability to compare and synthesize findings across different investigations and to generalize from these findings is obviously adversely affected.

THE NECESSITY FOR
CONCEPTUAL DEFINITIONS

It is an understatement to say that reality is complex. At the very least, reality consists of a multifaceted, dynamic flow of unique and unrepeatable events. The world at any given instant in time—and that includes everything in and on it—is never the same as the world at any other instant, either previous or subsequent. The water that flows at one particular instant or during any given day in the rivers of New Hampshire, the raindrops that fall on a particular evening in St. Louis, the expense account dinner that was eaten in New York are all unique and unrepeatable phenomena and events. Even the inanimate rock lying on the ground is unique. No two rocks are identical in terms of all their distinguishing characteristics—including time and space.

Yet we somehow manage to make sense out of this potentially dazzling and overwhelming amount of complexity. Very early in our lives we begin to apply our intellectual capacities to this dynamic, continuous flow of unique and unrepeatable events with a primary purpose of making it more manageable and avoiding being overwhelmed by it. We do this by defining, categorizing, and conceptualizing—by making abstractions and generalizations. Our language, indeed our very thinking, is permeated by such definitions, categories, and concepts. Without them, we could not function, except in a disjointed, "rediscovering-the-wheel" manner at each and every point in time. Without definitions, categories, and concepts, we could not communicate with others except in the most rudimentary of ways (see Bourne, 1966, pp. 1–2).

Consider the relatively simple concept "inanimate rock" used above. Quite obviously, the reader knew what was meant by the word *rock,* nor was it necessary to provide him with a description of the size, width, depth, crevices, markings, weight, density, mineral composition, and the like. No two rocks on the face of the earth are identical in every way. Yet the authors can write about rocks and the reader can comprehend and relate to what is written. Both the authors and the reader have a concept of what is meant by the word *rock;* moreover, our respective concepts are generally alike.

Concepts are basically abstractions. They involve grouping objects, phenomena, events, people, and so forth on the basis of one or more characteristics and disregarding all the other ways in which these objects differ (see Bourne, 1966, p. 1). Stated more concisely, concepts are abstractions based on the formation and use of categories to describe reality. Definitions are a basic form of categorization. They categorize by dichotomizing; that is, they state what *is* and what *is not* included in a particular category. Thus the terms *categorizing, classifying,* and *defining* are roughly synonomous and are here used interchangeably.

As implied above, categories serve many purposes (see Bruner, 1956; Plutchik, 1968). Categorizing enables us to make the immediate reality seem less complex and more manageable. Categorizing makes elements of our ongoing environment seem more familiar and reduces the need to learn new things each time the individual encounters another similar but not identical situation. In so doing, categories "generalize" from one situation to another, from one instant or case of reality to another. Categories also transcend immediate reality. They thus enable us to think and relate classes of objects and events to each other. Categorizing permits us to make judgments regarding the similarity or dissimilarity and appropriateness or inappropriateness of isolated events and specific phenomena. Finally, shared categories provide a fundamental basis for interpersonal communication.

Almost an infinite number of objects, phenomena, and events exist to be categorized, and each can be categorized in innumerable ways. Moreover, concepts are formed at different levels of abstraction. Forming concepts of tangible, denotable objects like "rocks" or "trees" is generally simpler than forming a concept of some less tangible phenomenon such as "love," "intelligence," or "personality." These latter concepts, which are abstractions of phenomena that are themselves abstract, are sometimes referred to as "constructs" (Selltiz et al., 1960, p. 41; Nunnally, 1967, p. 85). The scientific term *construct* simply means higher level (in terms of degree of abstraction) concepts.

Concepts and constructs are nothing more than labels or words that describe elements present in the everyday experience of virtually everyone. People are continuously engaged in developing and/or using concepts to contend with their reality. Even though they do not do so consciously and deliberately, they develop and use concepts and constructs in an attempt to organize and understand their world. Thus we all have some idea of what love is, even though it is quite difficult to point to love, to touch it, or to put it in a jar. We all have some idea of what intelligence is, or happiness, or personality. These concepts are generally held and understood and help shape and determine our interpretation of and reaction to reality.

Concepts (and the higher order concepts we call constructs) are thus at the core of human experience and furnish the foundation for human understanding and communication. Quite naturally, they are also the foundation of science, which, itself, is a human creation designed to further human understanding. As we have tried to indicate, concepts and constructs exist independent of science; that is, they would exist even if there were no such thing as science. Science enters the picture only when we wish to employ a formalized (in terms of structure and rigor) approach to the empirical development and use of concepts in the service of extending present knowledge and understanding. As is more thoroughly discussed below, extending knowledge involves integrating concepts and constructs into larger sets of interrelationships called theories.

Scientific research is a community enterprise (Selltiz et al., 1960, p. 44; Plutchik, 1968, p. 49). Each investigation rests on the methods and findings of earlier ones. To be able to relate findings from one investigation to another and to be able to generalize on the basis of specific findings require that research problems be formulated in abstract terms (Selltiz et al., 1960, pp. 46–47). It is hardly of any interest to the marketing manager to find out that 64 of the 86 women in a given study in Toledo, Ohio, consistently bought a single brand of toothpaste during the previous year. It may, however, be of tremendous significance to be able to classify (i.e., conceptualize) these people as working and nonworking women and to relate this to other research and perhaps arrive at the generalization that working women tend to be more brand loyal.

The object of scientific research—whether basic or applied—is to relate findings from the present investigation to those from other investigations so as to build a body of knowledge that permits generalization across instances. Without generalizations we would have to test each and every case to determine that a finding that held true in all previous cases also held true in this instance. Even those investigations whose purpose is to answer a specific and narrowly confined problem (i.e., those that have no interest in relating findings from a given study to other investigations or generalizing to similar situations) are based on procedures developed and findings obtained from earlier investigations. Thus, though generalization is not the intent in these cases, it provides the basis for conducting the highly applied single-shot investigation.

The ability to relate findings from one investigation to another and to generalize hinges, to a very great extent, on the clarity and precision with which concepts are defined. When concepts are not clearly and precisely defined, we increase the possibility of their being misunderstood, carelessly used, and improperly measured. Imprecise concepts tend to create confusion. They impede understanding and the development of general knowledge. "Naming is classifying. It is not necessary (or possible) that a naming scheme be best, but for effective communication, it is necessary that different people give the same name to the same objects" (Hartigan, 1975, p. 1). Many concepts have ultimately been discarded, not because they had no intrinsic utility, merit, or worth, but because so much imprecision existed regarding their assessment that it became no longer possible to communicate effectively regarding that concept.

Scientific concepts must be precisely and clearly defined to be useful (Carnap, 1950). If management is to become scientific, then it must also strive for precision in specifying concepts. This requires making explicit some of what is now implicit. Researchers of BL have always been guided by implicit conceptual definitions. The time has come to make these explicit. In the absence of explicit articulation, it is exceedingly difficult to see where areas of agreement and disagreement exist and to overcome the various problems inherent in the strictly operational approach.

A CONCEPTUAL DEFINITION
OF BRAND LOYALTY

Thus far we have argued that conceptual definitions are indispensable, that they must precede and guide the development of operational definitions, and that both definitions—particularly the former—must be as explicitly stated and precise as possible. A definition of BL is now provided to illustrate what we mean by a clear and precise definition.

The conceptual definition below was proposed in 1970 (Jacoby and Olson, 1970) and published one year later (Jacoby, 1971b). It has influenced conceptual definitions subsequently proposed by others, including those by Sheth and Park (1974) and Engel et al. (1973, pp. 550–552). Empirical substantiation for this definition was provided in 1973 (Jacoby and Kyner, 1973), although portions of the approach generated controversy (see Tarpey, 1974, 1975; Jacoby, 1975). Regardless, it remains the only full-scale conceptual definition to be subjected to rigorous empirical substantiation.

The definition is expressed by a set of six necessary and collectively sufficient conditions. These are that BL is (1) the biased (i.e., nonrandom), (2) behavioral response (i.e., purchase), (3) expressed over time, (4) by some decision-making unit, (5) with respect to one or more alternative brands out of a set of such brands, and (6) is a function of psychological (decision-making, evaluative) processes. A discussion of the significance of each of these conditions follows below.

More specifically, if BL were a random event, there would be no purpose in making it the object of applied scientific inquiry. Random events, though interesting, defy prediction, modification, and control. Without one or more of the latter three possibilities, there is no justification for expenditures of managerial time.

Verbal reports of bias (i.e., statements of preference or intention to buy) are insufficient for defining BL. Such loyalty requires that statements of bias be accompanied by biased purchasing behavior. A mother who repeatedly says that she likes Brand X disposable diapers better than any other available diaper and intends to buy some, but who always buys some other form or brand of diaper instead, is not brand loyal.

Nor does a single, biased behavioral act constitute BL. The term *loyalty* connotes a condition possessing some temporal duration, and it is therefore necessary to have the purchase act occur at at least two different points in time. Indeed, managerial interest is not and probably should not be in predicting the very next purchase. Rather, it is the pattern of purchases over time that is important. As is implicit in the sixth condition discussed below, brand-loyal individuals will, from time to time, compare their brands against other alternatives. This may involve the actual purchase and trial of one or more other brands. Predicting based on the five most recent purchases (all devoted to Brand X) that the consumer will purchase Brand X on the next occasion—when he actually ends up buying Brand Y—would not only result in a disconfirmed prediction but would also fail to incorporate the important fact that, for both theoretical (i.e., conceptual) and managerial reasons, BL is something expressed over time. It is not the *next* purchase event but the *pattern* of future purchase events that must be predicted for managerial success.

The phrase "decision-making unit" implies that the decision-maker need not be (a) the user or even the purchaser of the product, although he probably is, or (b) an individual; the decision-maker can be a collection of individuals (e.g., a family or organization). To illustrate proposition *a*, consider the husband, too busy to shop, who tells his wife what brand of shampoo to buy for him and whose wife obligingly does so time after time. It is he, the decision-maker (and, in this instance, the user as well), not she, the actual purchaser, who is brand loyal. As another example, assume that this husband decides his children should use Brand *X* toothpaste regularly despite their preferring Brand *Y*. Again, it is the father, not the purchaser-mother nor user-children, who is the brand-loyal decision-maker.

These distinctions are far from trivial. Consider their implications for both measurement and the search for BL correlates and determinants. It would probably be impossible to understand the psychological dynamics and causative factors underlying BL by using data collected on purchasers who are not also the decision-makers.

> For example, consider the husband, too busy to shop, who tells his wife what brand of shampoo to buy for him and she obligingly does so time after time. Assume, further, that this woman is participating in a consumer panel and dutifully records in her diary that, over 12 purchase trials, she purchased brand A 83.3% of the time (i.e., on 10 trials). Finally, assume that researchers now administer a personality instrument to this housewife-purchaser and find that she has a low need for dominance. Does it make any sense to then relate her dominance score to her percent-of-purchase score on the grounds that it will tell us something about *her* brand loyalty? It obviously is the husband who is brand loyal in this situation, not the wife who is only acting as the purchasing agent for the husband (Jacoby, 1975, p. 485).

Thus, of the three primary roles assumed by consumers—decision-maker, purchaser, user—it is only the first that is of consequence in attempts to understand the dynamics and causative factors underlying BL.

That the decision-making *unit* may entail more than one person also has important measurement implications. To understand adequately the psychodynamics involved, one must ensure that the measurements are based on all who take part in the decision-making process, particularly when the purchase represents a compromise. This could explain why individuals are sometimes not loyal (in their purchase behavior) to what they say is their most preferred brand (MPB).

The fifth condition--BL involves selecting one or more brands out of a set of brands—also has important implications. First, it recognizes that individuals can be and frequently are multibrand loyal, that is, loyal to two or more brands in the same product category (e.g., Duncan Hines and Pillsbury; Texaco, Shell Oil, and Citgo). This possibility did occur to early investigators (Brown, 1952–1953; Cunningham, 1956a) but has been more often ignored than explored. Recent exceptions are the empirical work of Massy, Frank, and Lodahl (1968), Ehrenberg and Goodhardt (1968), Jacoby (1969, 1970, 1971b), and the Howard and Sheth (1969) concept of "evoked set."

Second, BL is essentially a relational phenomenon. It describes preferential behavior toward one or more alternatives out of a larger field containing competing alternatives. Thus BL serves an acceptance-rejection function. Not only does it "select in" certain brands, it also "selects out" certain others. Before one can speak of being loyal, one must have the opportunity for being disloyal; there must be a choice. Consider the case of the ugliest man in the world who had the good fortune to find and marry the only woman in the world who would have him. The fact that he later cannot have the extramarital affair that he so strongly desires (because no other woman finds him appealing) does not mean he is "loyal" to his wife. Given the opportunity to express his disloyalty, he would. While practitioners are primarily

interested in the "select in" aspect of loyalty, scientific
inquiry and good managerial sense require that all
aspects of the phenomenon, including its inverse, be
studied to reach comprehensive understanding.

The sixth condition notes that BL is a function of decision-making, evaluative processes. It reflects a purchase decision in which the various brands have been
psychologically (perhaps even physically) compared and
evaluated on certain internalized criteria, the outcome of
this evaluation being that one or more brands was (were)
selected. Note that preference (such as is expressed in "I
like Brand X best" kinds of statements) is only one element in the evaluation process and is sometimes not the
most important. For example, price may dictate that
brand-loyal behavior be manifested toward *a* preferred
(or less preferred) brand (e.g., Cadillac) rather than *the
most* preferred brand (Rolls-Royce). Indeed, it is even
possible for BL to involve no positive affect toward the
selected alternative. Directing attention toward salient
evaluative decision criteria and away from the traditional
preference measures emphasizes that the psychological
processes underlying BL are insufficiently assessed by
simple "I like Brand X best" kinds of statements. Marketing researchers studying BL must identify the set of
salient evaluative criteria if they hope to provide answers
to questions regarding the underlying dynamics and
causes of BL.

As a result of this decision-making, evaluative process, the individual develops a degree of commitment to
the brand(s) in question; he is "loyal." The concept of
commitment provides an essential basis for distinguishing between brand loyalty and other forms of repeat purchasing behavior (RPB) and holds promise for assessing
the relative degrees of BL.*

The six criteria presented are considered necessary
and collectively sufficient for conceptually defining BL.

*Parenthetically, Pessemier's (1959) approach represents an interest-
ing way of operationalizing commitment.

Given, however, that we have an explicitly stated conceptual definition, what do we actually have? Where does it fit and how can it be used?

THE PLACE OF CONCEPTUAL DEFINITIONS IN FORMAL THEORY

As part of everyday experience, concepts (the result of abstracting, defining, and categorizing) enable us to cope with a reality that is simultaneously complex, dynamic, and unique. As part of the scientific endeavor, they serve the very same function. However, when a part of science, concepts are treated somewhat differently.

First, concepts in scientific usage become legitimate objects of scrutiny—items to be critically examined by the other members of the scientific community. Unlike vaguely defined concepts, explicitly stated ones enable others to criticize, and hence, these concepts highlight points of agreement and disagreement. This often leads to a clearer shared understanding of the essential core meaning of the concepts, although criticisms regarding the various side meanings often remain.

Second, as part of science, there is the inevitable move toward measuring and quantifying concepts. This process takes on a cyclical character, so that, with each iteration (i.e., from conceptual definition, to measurement, to conceptual definition), both the concept and measures of that concept are refined, made more precise, valid, reliable, useful, and so on.

Third, and perhaps most importantly, concepts become the building blocks of theory—and theory is the most powerful tool we have for efficiently acquiring and extending understanding. With theory, we can transcend the immediately observable and objectively tangible reality to arrive at more nearly comprehensive and deeper understanding of the phenomenon under consideration. It is theory that enables us to understand such things as forces we cannot see (e.g., gravity, motives) that control the behavior of things we can see (e.g., planets, people). It is theory that enables us to predict and subsequently locate things (e.g., planets) that had not previously been known to exist. It is theory that enables us to generalize. But at the very core of all theory we find concepts.

"*Any* abstraction from the observable facts is theoretical" (Ehrenberg, 1975, p. 161). Conceptual definitions—which are abstractions—are the essential building blocks of formal theory. Indeed, "concept formation and theory formation go hand in hand" (Kaplan, 1964, p. 32), and theory is more often than not defined as a set of logically interrelated concepts. The process of construct validation serves as the essential basis for the confirmation of theory.

> It is important to realize that all theories in science mainly concern statements about constructs rather than about specific, observable variables.... Scientists cannot do without constructs. Their theories are populated with them.... science is primarily concerned with developing measures of constructs and finding functional relations between measures of different constructs (Nunnally, 1967, p. 85).

Formal theory represents an attempt to gain increased understanding by bringing rigor and the conceptual tools of man (e.g., mathematics, logic, semantics) to bear on the issue to provide improved understanding. Scientific theories are often described in terms of the functions they serve. Although universal agreement does not exist on the matter, it does appear that we can speak in terms of at least six separate functions served by scientific theories. These are the descriptive, organizational, explanatory, predictive, communicative, and heuristic functions.

The *descriptive* function of theory refers to the fact that a basic purpose of theory is to identify the relevant phenomena and segregate them from what is unimportant. Identifying relevant phenomena and segregating the important from the unimportant require abstract conceptualization. Theories are networks of conceptual definitions, and it is at this most fundamental of levels that these definitions have a place in theory. Consider the following passage from Hall and Lindzey (1957, pp. 14–15).

> Another function which a theory should serve is that of preventing the observer from being dazzled by the full blown complexity of natural or concrete events. The theory is a set of blinders and it .... permits the observer to go about abstracting from the natural complexity in a systematic and efficient manner. Abstract and simplify he will, whether he uses a theory or not, but if he does not follow the guidelines of an explicit theory the principles determining his view will be hidden in implicit assumptions and attitudes of which he is unaware. The theory specifies to the user a limited number of more or less definite dimensions, variables, or parameters which are of crucial importance. The other aspects of the situation can to a certain extent be overlooked.

Because of the stereotype holding that hardnosed managers typically fail to find theory useful, we feel compelled to describe briefly the other functions of theory so that managers can perhaps better appreciate the relevance and value that theory holds for them.

Given that we have attended to the descriptive function (i.e., identified what we believe are the important aspects of reality to attend to), the next thing a theory must do is attend to the *organizational* function (i.e., attempt to indicate how these various aspects are related to one another). Such relationships may exist in time and/or space and are described symbolically (e.g., verbally, numerically, mechanically, graphically). Once we think we know what to pay attention to, we must begin to specify the framework for integrating these various factors.

The third and fourth functions served by theory typically generate the greatest amount of managerial interest. Given that one has described and organized the relevant portions of reality, one strives for higher levels of understanding through both *explanation* and *prediction*. While these two functions sometimes go hand in hand, they can operate independently. It is possible to explain how something happens (especially after the fact) but still be unable to predict just when it will occur. For example, early astronomers understood the reasons for eclipses and were even able to explain what happened to laypeople but, at the same time, were unable to predict when such eclipses would happen again. Con Edison, the New York utility company, seems to be having the same problem with respect to power failures. Conversely, the automobile driver stepping on the accelerator for the benefit of his mechanic might be able to predict with great accuracy what will occur when he steps down hard on the pedal (there will be a strange whirring sound in the engine) but be at a complete loss to explain why. Similarly, a marketing manager may be able to predict that sales of his product will go up if it is packaged in blue, but he may not have any understanding of the reason why. It is important for the manager to bear in mind, however, that both explanation and prediction require the prior explication of precise conceptual definitions.

Two final functions often ascribed to theories are the communicative and the heuristic. The *communicative* function simply means being able to describe complex phenomena in such a manner that others (perhaps limited to members of an in-group, such as a research community or group of managers) can easily and quickly understand what the speaker is talking about. The *heuristic* function simply means that the theory is capable of stimulating research necessary for determining its validity and extending its range of application.

The conceptual definition of BL provided above was primarily directed toward satisfying a descriptive function. In this regard the definition sought to distinguish BL from RPB, to indicate the significance of each and their relationship to each other, to outline explicitly the essential characteristics of BL, and to suggest guidelines for BL measurement. The definition was also able, however, to partially serve several other functions. First, by pointing to psychological commitment as the underlying causative dynamic, it began addressing the explanatory function. Second, to the extent that it has stimulated research that basically attests to its adequacy (see Jacoby and Kyner, 1973), it has obviously begun to satisfy the heuristic function. As of this point in time, no other conceptual definition has been subjected to such testing. Those that have been proposed remain theoretical. Third, in the process of specifying (a priori) and successfully confirming a series of hypothesized relationships, it began addressing the predictive function. Finally, since others have noted its influence on their own thinking and formulations regarding BL (see Engel, Kollat, and Blackwell, 1973; Sheth and Park, 1974), the definition would appear to be serving a communicative function. Under the circumstances it would appear that additional effort in regard to this definition would appear warranted and is likely to prove fruitful.

Several of the basic points we have been developing thus far may be summarized as follows. Being able to transcend the immediate situation and generalize to other, similar situations requires that we operate from an abstract conceptual structure called theory. The basic building blocks of theory (and of research) are concepts. To be maximally useful, concepts must be explicitly stated and precisely defined. Further, this conceptual explication must precede the collection of data so that it can guide measurement (operationalization) of the phenomenon under consideration. However, even after this is done, we still have one basic problem: How do we know that our concept or our measures of that concept are "right"? This brings us to a final necessary stage in the use of concepts in research, namely, the process by which we attempt to validate measures of concepts. This process, known as "construct validation," is the backbone of scientific research—both basic and applied.

CONSTRUCT VALIDATION: ENSURING THAT OUR MEASURES REFLECT OUR CONCEPTS

Given a precisely stated conceptual definition, it becomes possible to determine the extent to which a given operationalization adequately corresponds to and reflects that concept—totally, partially, or not at all. Such determination is sometimes made on a strictly logical basis. However, even if one is able to say that an operationalization (for example, the percent of purchases devoted to the most often purchased brand) seems to be a logical indicant of a concept (BL), one still has no basis for contending that this concept is itself a valid extrapolation from reality.

Actually, there are several basic types of validity, and the subject can quickly become quite complex. Figure 4.1 will assist us in an attempt to sort out these various types of validity in a manner that should be easily comprehended by most laypeople. Reading this figure from left to right implies that two supposedly distinct and nonoverlapping phenomena have been conceived (i.e., abstracted from reality) and given identity by way of labels. These two concepts are "brand loyalty" and "time pressure." In general, when one abstracts from reality and defines a concept, one does so because there is reason to believe, either on the basis of intuition or some prior conceptual framework (e.g., theory), that the concept is in some way important. Having two concepts implies that these may be meaningfully related to each other and that, by acquiring improved understanding of

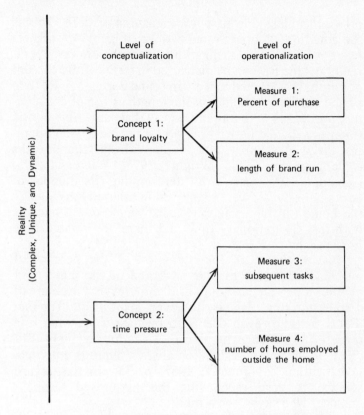

Question of interest: "What is the relationship between
time pressure and brand loyalty?"

Figure 4.1   Illustration of the relationship of reality to concepts and
measures

this interrelationship, it might be possible to improve
explanation, prediction, and/or control. Whether applied
or basic, all research "is concerned with establishing
functional relationships between variables" (Nunnally,
1967, p. 83).

However, "variables must be measured before they
can be related to one another" (Nunnally, 1967, p. 83).
That is, one cannot empirically relate BL to time

pressure unless one first has measures of both. This is the function of operationalizations. Figure 4.1 depicts two specific operationalizations for each concept. As already noted, BL can be measured in terms of the percent of purchases devoted to a given brand during a finite time period (Measure 1), and by the length of run of consecutive purchases of that brand during that same time period (Measure 2). Similarly, time pressures have been operationalized by (1) providing people with subsequent tasks to engage in (e.g., Wright, 1974; Winters, 1975; Chestnut, 1975) and (2) by determining the number of hours housewives were employed in salaried jobs outside the home (on the assumption that employment left one with less discretionary time and therefore created time pressures).

Just saying that something (be it the percent of purchases devoted to a given brand or the number of pebbles a person can count in 10 minutes) is a measure of a construct (e.g., BL) is, however, insufficient. The fact that a measure even seems to be measuring what it is reported to measure (i.e., has *face validity*) is still insufficient. In science, "validation always requires empirical investigation" (Nunnally, 1967, p. 75). In this regard science is very much like the hardnosed business manager who says "show me!"

"Before one can test the relationship between a specific trait [i.e., concept] and other traits, one must have confidence in one's measure of that trait" (Campbell and Fiske, 1959, p. 100). In other words, "for statements of relationship to have any meaning, each measure must . . . validly measure what it is purported to measure" (Nunnally, 1967, p. 83). What this means in terms of our example is that, before we can have any basis for taking a measure of BL and relating it to a measure of time pressure and then, on the basis of whatever we find, make statements regarding the relationship of BL and time pressure, we must be very certain that our measures of BL and of time pressure are indeed valid. This example brings us to the point where we can differentiate among the major types of validity and, on the basis of a consideration of these types, provide the rationale underlying the process employed to validate concepts.

Content validity refers to the special case in which a single measure is being related to a single denotable concept. Concepts vary in the degree to which the domain of content they refer to is concrete and directly observable. To the extent that the entire universe of elements is observable and can be concretely specified, we can determine the extent to which a given measure validly represents this specific universe of content (Cornbach, 1960; Nunnally, 1967). Generally, content validity is applied only in relation to tests and has little apparent utility in contemporary consumer research. We are not yet at the point where we can specify entire universes of directly observable content (although this actually may not be necessary, see Campbell, 1976, p. 198).

Criterion-related validity refers to the degree of relationship between a measure of one variable (say, Measure 1 in Figure 4.1) and a measure of a second variable (say, Measure 3 in Figure 4.1). Sometimes the labels *concurrent* and *predictive* validity are used, with the former reserved for instances in which the two measures are taken at the same time and the latter employed when one measure is taken and used to predict the second at some later point in time. Many of the validity coefficients referred to in consumer research are of the predictive-validity variety.

Demonstrating the existence of a high correlation by itself provides little or no understanding of the reasons for this relationship. One can have a predictive- (criterion-related) validity coefficient of .99 and still not know *why* it occurs or what it means—other than that scores on one measure are highly predictive of scores on a second. Indeed, the relationship may even be entirely meaningless. As one concrete example, Heeler and Ray (1972, p. 364) note that Kuehn (1963):

> improved the ability of the Edwards Personal Preference Schedule (EPPS) to predict car ownership.

He did it with EPPS scores computed by subtracting "affiliation" scores from "dominance"scores. Such a difference really has no psychological or marketing significance; it is just a mathematical manipulation that happened to work in one situation.

Furthermore, given that two measures (such as M_1 and M_3) had not earlier been demonstrated to be satisfactorily related to valid constructs (such as C_1 and C_2), then it is not legitimate to generalize from the data or measures in hand (see Selltiz et al., 1960, p. 164). In other words, all one could say in regard to the present example is that percent of purchase was related to number of hours worked, not that BL was related to time pressures.

Convergent validity represents the degree to which different operational measures of the same concept (e.g., Measures 1 and 2 in Figure 4.1) are highly intercorrelated. Assume we applied 10 different measures of BL to the same population. To the extent that these different measures are intercorrelated, we have greater confidence in the fact that each is an appropriate measure of the underlying construct. To the extent that they do not relate well to each other (i.e., the correlations are near zero), it may reflect that: (1) the measures are all poor and unsatisfactory and do not really measure anything at all: (2) each measure is doing a good job of measuring something, but a number of different things have been measured; and/or (3) the concept has been inadequately defined, and this has prevented the development of satisfactory measures. In any case low correlations between measures that supposedly address the same concept serve an important diagnostic function by telling us that our measures of the concept, or the concept itself, or both, are in need of refinement.

Of course, it may be that the concept, like the elephant being examined by seven blind men, is complex and has many different facets. Under these circumstances the measures may just be assessing different aspects of the same concept. Examples of such complex concepts (i.e., constructs) include intelligence, personality, life-style, and BL. When a concept is multifaceted, it requires a multifaceted measurement approach. Under these circumstances it is important to bear in mind the following: "Each measure should concern some one *thing,* some isolatable unitary attribute. To the extent that unitary attributes should be combined to form an overall appraisal ... [for example, BL], they should be rationally combined from different measures rather than haphazardly combined within one measure" (Nunnally, 1970, p. 8).

Factor analysis becomes a very important tool at this juncture (Nunnally, 1967, p. 101). For example, Olson and Jacoby (1971) applied 12 different operational measures of BL to the same subjects and were able to identify 4 relatively distinct factors explaining 67% of the common variance. These factors also emerged in several subsequent (unpublished) studies conducted by these authors. These data suggest that BL is a complex, multifaceted phenomenon that probably cannot be adequately measured by a single indicant.

In the absence of consistently high positive correlations between different measures of the same construct, there is no justifiable basis for contending that either was indeed a measure of the underlying construct (unless, of course, there is evidence that one of these measures does correlate highly with yet other indices previously demonstrated to be satisfactory indicants of the concept, i.e., criterion validity). That is, given that Measures 1 and 2 have not been shown to be highly interrelated to each other, we have no justification for relating either one to measures of another concept if our objective is to be able to make statements regarding the relationship between the two concepts. Not much data exist to indicate what the interrelationships are between and among the different loyalty indices, and there are reasons to believe that the convergent validity across many of these indices might be very low. Moreover, while high intercorrelation between different measures of the same concept is necessary, it is still not sufficient.

Construct validity is the ultimate validity insofar as scientific research is concerned. It refers to procedures by which evidence is obtained to show that the measures we have developed are indeed valid indicants of the concept we have in mind, that is, that they measure what we say they measure. According to Kerlinger (1964, p. 448): "Scientifically speaking, construct validity is one of the most significant advances of modern measurement theory and practice."

Given that we have already articulated a precise conceptual definition, the process of construct validation involves demonstrating that different operational measures of this construct (1) are internally consistent (i.e., highly intercorrelated, demonstrating a high degree of convergent validity) and (2) relate as expected to other variables. Nunnally describes internal consistency as the degree to

> which different measures in a domain tend to supply the same information [tend to correlate highly with one another and be similarly affected by experimental treatments]. To the extent that the elements of such a domain show this consistency, it can be said that *some* construct may be employed to account for the data, but it is by no means sure that it is legitimate to employ the construct name which motivated the research. In other words, consistency is a *necessary* but not *sufficient* condition for construct validity.... sufficient evidence for construct validity is that the supposed measures of the construct (either a single measure of observables or a combination of such measures) *behave as expected.* (1967, p. 92).

The test of how well different supposed measures of a construct "go together" is the extent to which they have similar curves of relationship with a variety of treatment variables. It does not matter what the form of the relationship is . . . as long as the supposed measures of the construct behave similarly. . . . When a variety of measures behave similarly in this way over a variety of experimental treatments, it becomes meaningful to speak of them as measuring a construct (Nunnally, 1967, pp. 90–91).

Our example in Figure 4.1 would have to be expanded to include other concepts and measures to provide a clearer indication of construct validity. The gist of the approach is, however, to ensure that the purported measures of a given construct (say, BL) are highly related to each other (i.e., show high convergent validity), while at the same time they correlate as predicted (be it positively, negatively, or not at all) with valid measures of other constructs. As a hypothetical example, we might have good reason to believe that BL was positively related to time pressures, negatively related to size of family, and independent of size of community. Under these circumstances we would want *both* of our measures of BL (in Figure 4.1) to be highly correlated with each other, positively correlated with time pressures, negatively correlated with size of family, and uncorrelated with size of community.

  Several important considerations surround efforts to establish construct validity (see Campbell, 1976; Cook and Campbell, 1976; and Nunnally, 1970). Some of the more important of these are as follows. First, establishing construct validity for the measures of a given construct requires that we have several measures (or "exemplars") of that construct. "They should demonstrably share common variance attributable to the target construct and should also differ from each other in unique ways that are irrelevant to the target construct" (Cook and Campbell, 1976, p. 239). Second, it is necessary that the various measures of the construct be more highly correlated with each other than they are with measures of any other construct to which they are supposedly related. In the example provided above, this would necessitate that our two measures of BL (M_1 and M_2) demonstrate a higher correlation with each other than either did with either of the measures of time pressure (M_3 and M_4). Third, "more construct validity can be attributed to the instrument to the extent that the hypotheses being tested are nonoverlapping" (Campbell, 1976, p. 203). That is: "Numerous successful predictions dealing with . . . diverse 'criteria' give greater weight to the claim of construct validity than do . . . predictions involving very similar behavior" (Cronbach and Meehl, 1955, p. 295).

Though a formal procedure for establishing construct validity has been available for nearly two decades (Campbell and Fiske, 1959), no report of its application to BL exists in the literature. However, while the rigorous procedures outlined by Campbell and Fiske are, at least as of this point in time, the most satisfactory for demonstrating construct validity, the few investigations that have incorporated multiple measures of BL in the same study offer some potential for demonstrating construct validity. The Jacoby and Kyner (1973) study provides an example. First, an attempt was made to articulate explicitly and precisely a conceptual definition of BL. Second, an experimental situation was set up to manipulate variables in such a way as to provide opportunities for both loyalty and disloyalty. Third, a series of seven different operationalizations supposedly indicative of different aspects of BL as conceived were used to determine whether loyalty and/or disloyalty were generated as hypothesized. Six out of the seven measures were highly intercorrelated and appeared to "hang together" and behave (i.e., provide results) as predicted: 17 out of 18 relationships based on these 6 measures were significant as predicted (16 of the 17 being significant at $p < .01$); similarly, 17 out of 18 predictions of nonsignificance were confirmed.

The essence of this chapter has been to call attention to the fact that, while BL remains an intriguing concept with tremendous potential for managerial application, none of this potential can be realized until we have valid measures of BL. Procedures for developing such measures are available but not used. These consist of first attempting to state precisely what we believe BL is and is not, that is, developing a conceptual definition. Next, this involves developing measures that supposedly assess the concept (or different facets of the concept) as defined, that is, developing apparently suitable operational definitions. Finally it is necessary to engage in empirical research to demonstrate that our measures do indeed match our concepts (i.e., construct validation). It is only after these procedures are followed (and we have satisfactorily valid measures of BL) that we can begin to use these measures to evaluate the relationships between BL and other variables of managerial concern.

In other words, successful use of BL in the applied managerial context must await the development of satisfactory measures. No other course is open to us, other than those that would necessarily include misinterpretation and misapplication. It is, however, possible to speculate just how and where satisfactory measures of BL could be used by marketing managers once they were developed. Chapter 5 adopts such a perspective.

FIVE

AREAS FOR

Marketing Applications

INVOLVING

Brand Loyalty Measurement

Once satisfactory brand loyalty (BL) indices have been developed, we can turn to the task of identifying information and findings of relevance to the practitioner. Since BL and repeat purchasing behavior (RPB) are inextricably involved with developing, maintaining, and increasing market share, this becomes a particularly worthwhile endeavor.*

*This monograph was originally prepared in fulfillment of a contract with a major consumer product firm. While this firm has very generously permitted the vast majority of the original monograph to

101

MARKET SHARE, MARKET SEGMENTS, AND BRAND LOYALTY

At any given point in time, a brand's market share is generally composed of (1) those people who are (perhaps loyal) repeat purchasers of that brand, (2) those people who are only occasional purchasers of that brand, and (3) those who are trying that brand for the first time. From the marketer's perspective, it is important to consider what makes people repeat purchasers of his brand and what makes people switch either from or to his brand. The marketer interested in increasing a brand's market share will want to ensure that his repeat purchasers remain repeat purchasers of his brand and will attempt to induce individuals who are either repeat purchasers of other brands, or who are not repeat purchasers of any particular brand but do make purchases in the product category, to switch to his brand and, once having switched, to become repeat purchasers. It can thus be said that the development and maintenance of RPB and the inducing of brand switching are at the core of effective marketing.

Figure 5.1 organizes these market segments into an overall framework. It begins by noting that, at any given instant, the market contains two primary segments: those individuals who have purchased Brand *A* and those who have not.

The *nonpurchasers* of Brand *A* may be subdivided into (1) those who do not make purchases in this product category, (2) those who do make purchases of this product but are neither loyal nor repeat purchasers of any single brand, and (3) those who are purchasers of the product and who are either loyal or repeat purchasers of some other brand(s).

---

be released for publication, it did request that several portions of the report bearing directly on applications not be divulged. As a result this chapter can only begin to hint at the numerous opportunities for enhancing market share.

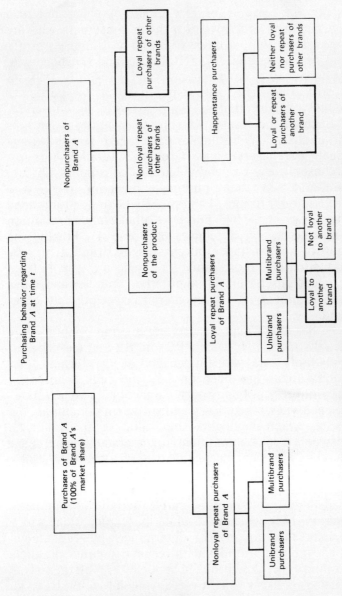

Figure 5.1 The market share for Brand A at time t segmented according to purchaser behavior

The *purchasers* (i.e., market share) of Brand A may be segmented as follows: (1) those consumers who are nonloyal repeat purchasers of Brand A; (2) those who are loyal repeat purchasers of Brand A; and (3) those who just happened to have bought Brand A recently, perhaps the last time they made a purchase in this particular product category, that is, "happenstance" purchasers.

Each of the three segments constituting Brand A's market share may be further partitioned. Group 1 (loyal repeat purchasers) and Group 2 (nonloyal repeat purchasers) may be subdivided into consumers who are unibranded in their purchase behavior (i.e., who purchase only Brand A) and those who are multibranded buyers (i.e., those who purchase other brands in addition to making regular purchases of Brand A). Finally, the group of happenstance purchasers of Brand A may be subdivided into those individuals who are usually loyal or repeat purchasers of some other brand(s) and those who are not loyal or repeat purchasers of any other brand.

As noted in Chapter 1 and amplified in Chapter 4, we see a distinction between RPB and BL and view the latter as only one specific variety of the former. Our primary focus has been on BL (the cells denoted by heavy borders in Figure 5.1). Conceptually we define its presence via six necessary and sufficient conditions, the last of which highlights the value of psychological constructs (e.g., commitment) in understanding purchase behavior. The mere suggestion of such a construct is not, however, enough. If BL is ever to be managed, not just measured, it will have to be elaborated in a much more detailed description of cognitive activities. As Massy (1966, p. 172) observes, "while an 'explanation' which suggests that loyalty is determined by consumers' knowledge and attitudes with respect to either products or brands (perhaps brought about by the effects of advertising) is likely to be true, any such hypothesis is devoid of theoretical content unless it seeks to explain how these attitudes come into being. . . ."

What then are the psychological steps in the development of BL? How are these steps reflected (perhaps even maintained) by the decision-making activities surrounding brand choice? Our attempt in this last chapter is to begin to answer these questions in terms of a theoretical perspective.

For management objectives this perspective has two major areas of application. First, it suggests the types of marketing information needed before informed decisions regarding BL can be made. Second, it points out the targets at which intervention techniques might be aimed. That is, if we are ever to effectively promote or inhibit the development of BL, marketing activities must be directed at the appropriate variables.

Although only one general process of development is described, note that the segmentation scheme (Figure 5.1) defines the existence of four specific contexts in which this process might operate. A successful marketing strategy would be one in which all four contexts are considered. This calls for the analysis of not one but of all major brands receiving some degree of RPB.

A THEORETICAL PERSPECTIVE ON THE DEVELOPMENT OF BRAND LOYALTY

Consumer research has become increasingly tied to a paradigm emerging from experimental/cognitive psychology. Its primary influence has been on the marketing sciences' interpretation of decision-making or choice activities, and one of its more popular labels has been that of "information processing." As stated by Hughes (1974, p. 3), "Information processing research is rapidly becoming an accepted way of examining how a buyer or a consumer chooses among the many products, services, and brands that are available on the marketplace."

Although the inclusion of this perspective came quite early in the development of marketing models (e.g., Nicosia, 1966; Howard and Sheth, 1969), recent developments have gone into considerably more detail. Methods have improved in their general level of sophistication with the result that hard empirical data are beginning to accumulate. For a bibliography of this research the reader is referred to a compilation by Olson and Muderrisoglu (1977). A sampling of some of the latest references includes Payne, 1976; Wright and Barbour, 1977; Howard, 1977; Chestnut and Jacoby, 1977; Bettman, in preparation; Jacoby and Chestnut, in preparation.

The central idea underlying this paradigm is quite simple. In brief, it contends that ". . . a number of mental operations, called processing stages, occur between stimulus and response" (Massaro, 1975, p. 19). The stimulus in this case is the brand and the response is the overt behavior of choice. An information-processing perspective poses the question: What are the number and nature of stages that intervene in the mind of the consumer?

The analysis of stages begins by conceptualizing the stimulus itself (i.e., the brand) as a complex body of information (cf. Jacoby and Chestnut, 1977). This information is selectively acquired into the decision-making system (i.e., the consumer) and then passed sequentially from one processing stage to another. "The operations of a particular stage take time and transform the information in some way, making the transformed information available to the following stage of processing" (Massaro, 1975, p. 20). This chain of activities continues until at some point a conscious choice of brand is made and then implemented through the physical actions surrounding purchase.

There are many ways in which the external representation of the brand and its shopping environment (i.e., stimuli as defined by the marketer) can be transformed in the process of making a decision. One method, which may indeed by inescapable (i.e., auto-

matic—especially with regard to frequently purchased
nondurables), is that of merging information from the environment with brand-related information available from
long-term memory. This is no more than observing that
consumers acquire purchasing experience (from the
input of advertising, previous consumption, word-of-
mouth communication, etc.) and actively use this
experience in selecting brands. Most marketing practitioners and academicians would readily accept this
observation. Unfortunately, few have any great understanding of exactly how and with what result this process
might take place. "It is our observation that people
working in the consumer area have very naive concepts
and little curiosity about how the person organizes the
cognitive space in which experience with and communications about products are stored and from which
considerations affecting purchasing choices are drawn"
(McGuire, 1976, p. 310).

Our brief account of an information-processing
perspective on BL attempts to dispel some measure of
this naiveté by focusing on the impact of previously
stored information in purchasing. In evaluating this
perspective, the reader should be warned against posi-
tioning its ideas in terms of a full-scale theory. This is not
our intention. Rather, we would hope only to suggest the
directions in which we should take such a theory.

The perspective begins by restricting its attention to
one general stage of cognitive activity: that of conscious
decision-making (cf. Chestnut and Jacoby, 1977).
Theorists (e.g., Massaro, 1975, p. 20) frequently distinguish between two aspects of a stage: its "structures"
and its "functions." Structures would refer to content,
the elements of information existing within the stage at
some point in time. Functions would refer to the actual
processing, the procedures or mechanisms by which
such informational elements are used in arriving at a decision.

With regard to BL the following three specific structures of information can be examined: beliefs, states of
affect, and behavioral intentions. The focus here is on

brand-specific structures that (upon their retrieval from long-term memory) may influence purchasing. For example, a consumer might acquire and then at point of purchase recall a strong positive feeling (i.e., state of affect) toward a given brand. This would enter into the conscious evaluation of the stimulus environment and might well result in the purchase of that brand.

Two major points should be made concerning these structures. First, they are all types of information that *by themselves* can determine the brand chosen and, to some extent, the repeated choice of the same brand. Second, they are suggestive of an underlying continuum of learning. Along these lines a tentative hierarchy is proposed. Consumers can be conceived as first acquiring beliefs (if in nothing more than the fact the brand exists), then forming states of affect (feelings conditioned over time by experience), and finally establishing explicit intentions to behave.

Returning to the example of Brand *A*, we might consider its repeat purchasers in terms of the steps in this hierarchy. Figure 5.2 is a Venn diagram that suggests the

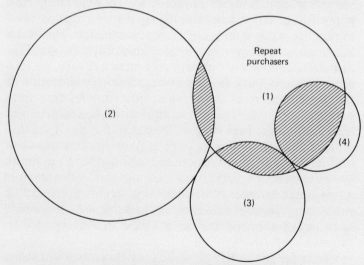

Repeat purchasers

(2)

(1)

(4)

(3)

Figure 5.2 Venn diagram of sets of Brand *A* purchasers

existence of four distinct sets of Brand *A* purchasers. Set 1 is central to the diagram and represents, by definition, all those purchasers who through some behavioral criterion can be classified as repeat purchasers of Brand *A*. Sets 2, 3, and 4 are composed of those who continue to purchase the product and whose selection(s) of Brand *A* can be traced back to one of three causes (i.e., beliefs, affect, or intentions). As depicted, these sets are assumed to be independent. This is not to suggest, for example, that those selecting Brand *A* because of liking or affect lack beliefs. Rather, it implies only that affect was the primary cause underlying the Brand *A* purchasing. Clearly, each of these three sets has the potential of overlapping with Set 1. That is, their members may engage in some degree of behavioral consistency over time. This warrants a closer inspection of the sets and their relationships.

Set 2 consists of those purchasers who selected Brand *A* because of a positive belief (or set of beliefs) regarding the brand. A belief can be defined in terms of a high subjective probability estimate on the part of the consumer attaching the object (i.e., the brand) to some attribute (cf. Fishbein and Ajzen, 1975, p. 12). For example, a consumer might believe that a particular brand of margarine has a highly desirable flavor. This connection between brand and flavor would enter into the conscious evaluation of the stimulus environment (along with external information on price, relative size, package types, etc.) and result in an increased likelihood of selecting the "best tasting" brand.

Set 3 consists of those purchasers whose continued experience with or beliefs about the brand have led to the establishment of some state of positive affective response (cf. Byrne, 1971). There is a growing body of evidence to suggest that states of affect (i.e., the positive or negative feelings that one associates with a given stimulus) can have a substantial influence in directing behavior. "In general, individuals will move (physically, verbally, or symbolically) toward those they like and away from those they dislike" (Byrne and Griffitt, 1973, p. 325). Although these purchasers may still use information obtained from the environment or from their own beliefs, their primary rationale will be one of attraction or liking.

Set 4 consists of those purchasers who selected Brand A because of an explicit intention to be loyal (i.e., consistent) purchasers of that brand. A behavioral intention can be defined in a way similar to that of beliefs in that it attaches a high subjective probability to the association of an object with a behavior or, in this case, a series of future behaviors (cf. Fishbein and Ajzen, 1975, p. 12). As an information structure this final element in the learning process would have the most direct impact on brand choice. It would restrict the consumer in no uncertain terms to a particular brand's warranting repeat purchase.

Having defined these four sets, we proceed by considering their relationships. One important characteristic of the diagram centers on the percent to which sets 2, 3, and 4 overlap with the phenomenon of repeat purchase. This percent of overlap steadily increases from a low in terms of belief-directed purchasing to a high in terms of intention-directed purchasing.

Only a relatively small percent of those buying Brand A because of a belief associate themselves with RPB. Given the vast quantity of information to which they are constantly exposed, consumers are bound to develop a variety of different beliefs. Although a positive belief regarding Brand A might be instrumental in generating an individual purchase, its ability to win out over other brand-related beliefs is likely to vary over time. Furthermore, the belief itself is often transitory, susceptible to the advertising and promotional efforts of other brands.

Affect-directed purchasing should exhibit a much greater degree of overlap. Brand preferences (i.e., liking) are more enduring than beliefs and may well influence decision-making activities on qualitatively different levels. For example, beyond serving as a viable rationale for the purchase of Brand A, a brand preference might direct the acquisition of information contained in the environment. This could be in terms of search behavior or even selective perception. Current research findings suggest (cf. Chestnut, 1977; Jacoby and Chestnut, 1977) that liked alternatives gain easier access to the consumer's "evoked set" (cf. Howard and Sheth, 1969, p. 27). This bias is likely to reduce the variance in externally derived information and, thereby, the potential for brand switching.

The greatest percent of overlap should, however, occur in the case of set 4. These purchasers have reduced the elements of belief and affect into a simple intention to behave. They store a decision rule that directs the purchasing of Brand A. More importantly, they reflect loyal purchasers in that their rule may well include an explicit statement of repurchase. Brand A is the "best" that will ever occur on the market. Hence, why look further? There will of course be instances of occasional switching (e.g., out-of-stock conditions or a hurried mistake of brand identity), but this should represent only a small fraction of set 4's purchasing.

Although the percent of overlap increases as beliefs lead to affect and affect in turn leads to behavioral intentions, another implication of the learning assumption should be noted. Given that Brand A has good qualities, many of its purchasers (if not all) will develop one or another positive beliefs. These may influence purchasing and, in some cases, repeat purchasing. Positive beliefs need not, however, result in the development of a brand preference or general state of positive affect. Only through many such beliefs and repeated experience with the brand will some members of set 2 proceed into set 3. Likewise, not all those in set 3 will elaborate their "liking" of Brand A with an intention to repurchase. Many of those in set 3 will accept brand switching in search of variety or economy or as a result of impulse. Those finally entering set 4 will have a distinct and compelling reason for doing so. The net result of this filtration process is that of a decline in set size (2, 3, 4). As depicted in Figure 5.2, this may decrease the actual number of repeat purchasers (and thus the marketing importance) in each area of overlap.

In summary, BL can be thought of as the portion of RPB that finds a basis in terms of internally stored structures of information: brand-related beliefs, states of affect, and behavioral intentions. Clearly, the representation offered in Figure 5.2 is somewhat idealized. It is easy to imagine a situation in which set 1 would be relatively small or in which sets 3 and 4 would not yet have formed. Our graphic intent in this figure was more for illustration than for modeling.

Note also that we take no particular credit for being the sole "originators" of these ideas. Intimations of these structures have existed in the marketing literature since the very beginnings of an interest in BL. Copeland (1923), for example, observed that "when a manufacturer undertakes to focus the potential demand on his product with brand identification, he must consider the attitude with which the consumer ordinarily approaches the purchases of such an article. The attitude of the consumer may be (1) recognition, (2) preference, or (3) insistence" (p. 287). He would seem to suggest that the intersection of set 1 with sets 2, 3, and 4 is to some degree a function of product class.

In more recent years a number of different consumer theorists (e.g., Jacoby, 1969; Day, 1969; Jacoby and Kyner, 1973; Sheth and Park, 1974; Wind, 1975) have adopted the thesis that attitudinal and behavioral BL must be separated to be properly understood. This would seem to be at the very core of our perspective.

The perspective would be incomplete, however, if it did not go beyond a consideration of information structures. As we mentioned at the outset, an information-processing stage also includes some number of functions. These operate on the structures to produce brand choice. With regard to RPB one variety of conscious decision-making function merits special attention. This is what has come to be known as the "decision heuristic."

Heuristics are sets of rules or procedures that a consumer might use in narrowing the field of brand alternatives. They are not what one might usually think of in terms of a thorough comparison and then integration of product attributes. Their primary value lies in the ability to reduce the costs of search via a relatively quick recognition of what must eventually decide choice behavior. As discussed by Braunstein (1976):

> The use of a class of procedures by human subjects that usually, but not always, achieves correct solutions is one of the most important findings in the study of problem-solving. . . . The current usage of the term "heuristic" is based on a definition offered by Polya (1945) in the context of theorem proving: "Heuristic reasoning is reasoning not regarded as final and strict but as provisional and plausible only, whose purpose is to discover the solution of the present problem" (p. 113). In the context of problem-solving, heuristic processes can be defined as problem-solving methods that tend to produce efficient solutions to difficult problems by restricting the search through the space of possible solutions (pp. 154–155).

Brand choice is often a matter of finding a ready solution to a somewhat difficult problem. This may in many cases entail the use of memory and "a strong tendency to summarize past experience in terms of a 'representative' or 'average' case" (Posner, 1973, p. 81). Consider the everyday purchase situation of selecting a brand of breakfast cereal. Studies (cf. Jacoby and Chestnut, 1977) indicate that a majority of consumers adopt what might be termed a "satisficing" posture in making this decision. That is, they maintain no real intention of finding the "best" brand in what would necessarily involve a complex evaluation of some 40 to 50 alternatives. Rather, they attempt only to locate the one brand that will meet their basic requirements. This is by no means a final or strict solution to the problem of brand choice. In its heuristic approximation of the "correct" solution, it

might often result in an undesirable purchase. The consequences of this would not, however, be great in that the
product is low in cost and short in duration.

One obvious procedure for locating this satisfactory
brand is that of a complete reliance on brand name. The
choice by brand name heuristic (cf. Jacoby, Chestnut,
Weigl, and Fisher, 1976; Bettman and Jacoby, 1976) has
two major benefits. First, it minimizes the cost of both
time and effort. In most categories of packaged goods,
brand names are visually accessible and easily recognized through an elaboration of logo, colors, and
the like. Second, for the acquisition of a single cue, brand
name maximizes the pool of available information. That
is, it recalls a variety of information structures that have
been "chunked" under the tag of one particular name
(cf. Jacoby, Szybillo, and Busato-Schach, 1977).

The importance of the brand name heuristic as a
loyalty-promoting function resides in its ability to ex-
clude automatically all external sources of information
at point of purchase. Beliefs, states of affect, and behavioral intentions enter uncontested as the basic ra-
tionales for choice. Used within this context, their relationship to RPB can only be enhanced. The question
now arises: With what frequency and under what conditions are brand name choice heuristics actually applied?

In behavioral simulations of nondurable purchase Jacoby and Chestnut (1977) provide the beginnings of an
answer. Recreating all the necessary components of the
purchasing environment (e.g., motivation, package information, subject-controlled selectivity), they attempt
to monitor the process of information acquisition. This
includes the exact number, type, and order of values acquired. The results are striking. "approximately 60%
($\pm 5\%$) of the subjects in the three Brand Name Present
(BNP) conditions engaged in some information acquisition behavior prior to making their decision" (Jacoby
and Chestnut, 1977, p. 83). For the three product classes
of breakfast cereal, margarine, and headache remedies,
this meant that nearly 40% of the consumers tested (sam-

ples ranging in size from 104 to 198) made their decision via an immediate selection of brand name. They did not stop to consider pricing, package size, nutrient value, and other features. They went directly to a familiar name and on the basis of recalled associations implemented purchase. Post-task measures of certainty, if anything, showed that those engaging in search were less certain of their choice than those looking only to brand name.

These results are in the context of a single purchase decision. It might be argued that for most nondurable purchasing this is atypical. Products such as breakfast cereal are usually purchased during a shopping trip involving a number of sequential purchasing activities. In an attempt to simulate the growing time costs of search activity in a multiple-decision task, Chestnut (1975) had subjects engage in varying numbers of simulated purchase decisions (either 1, 4, 8, or 12 products). With an increasing number of decisions the incidence of choice by brand name increased significantly. Thus, under more real-life conditions, the heuristic use of past experience gained even greater influence.

To summarize, an information-processing perspective on BL should include an explication of both structures and functions. If we focus on a consumer's more conscious decision-making activities, three basic structures (i.e., beliefs, states of affect, and behavioral intentions) and one specific function (i.e., the choice by brand name heuristic) would seem to merit further attention.

AREAS OF MARKETING APPLICATIONS

As previously noted, operating on BL so as to increase a brand's market share will require both the collection of marketing information on a variety of factors and the targeting of intervention techniques at the appropriate causative variables. In relation to these goals our theoretical perspective sheds light on (1) the distinguishing characteristics of loyal purchasers, (2) the psychological reasons underlying their purchase behavior, (3) the purchase- and usage-related behaviors engaged in by individuals during and subsequent to purchase, and (4) the factors likely to induce some amount of brand switching.

The distinguishing characteristics that should be examined include the standard socioeconomic and demographic factors, as well as a wide variety of social (e.g., opinion leadership) and individual difference factors. Are there tendencies for individuals with certain socioeconomic, demographic, or psychological characteristics to be more or less loyal? Despite mixed findings regarding the tendency to be brand loyal across different product categories (i.e., "general" BL), it is quite possible that, with improved BL measures, characteristics could be identified that would relate to general BL tendencies. There already is evidence to suggest that having little time (as is the case with the working wife, e.g., Anderson, 1972; Carman, 1970; Jacoby, Olson, and Szybillo, 1971) tends to be associated with higher levels of BL. Other evidence suggests that older people tend to be more brand loyal (Day, 1969; Engel, Kollat, and Blackwell, 1968, p. 583; Geiselman, 1970; Lamont and Rothe, 1971; McHale, 1971; Newman and Werbel, 1973). Certain implications for promotional and advertising strategies (in terms of segmentation and advertising themes) seem apparent in these findings.

The reasons underlying purchase or nonpurchase of Brand A (versus purchase or nonpurchase of some other brand) need to be studied in depth, these reasons being categorized into whether they are causative or contributory. (Causative reasons are those that are sufficient to determine behavior by themselves; contributory reasons exert influence on behavior but do not determine behavior by themselves.) The literature in psychology on information processing and especially on commitment (Kiesler, 1968, 1971) would appear to provide several interesting directions for application.

The findings that both consumers with relatively little free time for shopping (e.g., working wives), as well as consumers with relatively large amounts of discretionary time available for shopping (the elderly), tend to be .highly loyal suggest that people can be and probably are loyal for a wide variety of reasons. Can we separate these reasons empirically and measure their impact on purchasing? Relatedly, can we examine their psychological dynamics? Again, the literature on the subject of commitment and information processing should prove fruitful in this regard.

There seem to be sufficient data to suggest that individuals who perceive large interbrand differences in quality tend to be brand loyal (e.g., Anderson, 1974; Jacoby, 1971b; Jacoby, Olson, and Szybillo, 1971; Lamont and Rothe, 1971. McConnell, 1968b; Olson and Jacoby, 1972). One implication to be derived is that promotions designed to foster BL might do well to incorporate quality and quality-related themes. Questions that arise are: Is the perception of a brand's overall quality the influential factor, or is it perceived quality regarding one or two specific attributes of that brand? What determines the consumer's selection of one high-quality brand over another brand of equally high perceived quality? Perhaps more basically, what determines the consumer's perceptions of quality and quality differences? Research has shown that perceived worth (i.e., perceived value for the money) may be more directly related than perceived quality to actual purchase behavior (Shapiro, 1970; Szybillo and Jacoby, 1974). Therefore, the factors leading to judgments of perceived worth should also be examined.

Related prepurchase and postpurchase behaviors include such things as the nature of the brand evaluations these consumers engage in, the word-of-mouth communications they engage in, their media viewing and reading habits, and so on. Related purchase behaviors include the frequency and quantity purchased, the store in which purchase takes place, and so on.

Other than the fact that people who are brand loyal tend to confine their purchases to one (or a limited

number of) brand(s), are there other differences in their
behavior? Specific questions include the following. Do
loyal consumers tend to be people who buy the product
in larger or smaller amounts than nonloyal consumers?
Can they be persuaded to buy and use more of the
product than they are already using? What factors
increase or decrease the strength of BL? Are there differences in frequency of purchase between loyal and
nonloyal consumers? Are there differences in the way
they use and/or dispose of the product (see Jacoby, Berning, and Dietvorst, 1977)?

Do brand-loyal consumers engage in different kinds
of behaviors—relating to the acquisition, evaluation, and
transmission of information—than nonloyal consumers
do? For example, what are the media viewing and reading habits of loyal versus nonloyal consumers? Do loyal
consumers engage in word-of-mouth conversations regarding those brands to which they are loyal? If so, what
is the nature and content of these conversations? If the
content is positive from the marketer's perspective, how
can he stimulate such word-of-mouth activity? Do brand-
loyal consumers process information differently from
product package panels, package inserts, and advertise-
ments? In particular, do brand-loyal consumers look for
and attend to different types of package and advertising
information than nonloyal consumers do? Preliminary
evidence (Jacoby, Chestnut, Weigl, and Fisher, 1976, pp.
311–312; Jacoby, Chestnut, and Fisher, 1977) suggest
that they do. Numerous possibilities would probably
open up for effective promotional efforts, given a more
detailed understanding of how brand-loyal consumers
differ from nonloyal consumers in regard to information-
processing strategies.

On the assumption that a person is a repeat purchaser
of our brand, there are more opportunities to reach him
with special promotional materials inserted in (and on)
the product's package. What are the best approaches for
exploiting these opportunities? Relatedly, should separate advertising campaigns be devised and directed

toward people already purchasing (and perhaps loyal to) our brand and toward those who have only occasionally or perhaps never purchased our brand?

This brings us to the issue of brand switching. Just what factors cause brand switching? Is it more a function of dissatisfaction with one's current brand, or is it the attraction promised by a competing new brand that generates the switching behavior? Are certain kinds of people more prone to switching than others? What kinds of promotional appeals and strategies are most likely to induce brand switching? Conversely, and equally important, what kinds of strategies and tactics can be successfully employed to make loyal purchasers of our brand relatively immune to the brand-switching inducements of others? McGuire (1969) describes a dozen approaches for producing resistance to persuasion. How can these be applied by the marketing manager for Brand *A*? How can these be foiled by this same manager when they are used in behalf of Brand *B*?

CONCLUSION

Our conclusion is brief. Despite more than 300 published studies, BL research is kept afloat more because of promise than results. A basic reason for the lack of any solid contribution is the exceedingly naive approach to BL measurement. Unfortunately, it is all too often true that all one has to do is label something a measure of BL and it is automatically accepted as such by journal editors, reviewers, and even knowledgeable marketing managers. Attempts to demonstrate the adequacy of BL measures are virtually nonexistent. Our critical faculties, which often operate with respect to all kinds of other phenomena and data, are strangely quiescent when it comes to considering BL research.

The potential of the concept to prove valuable in terms of reaching applied marketing objectives more than justifies the relatively negligible time, effort, and expense required to conduct the necessary developmental work with regard to measurement. We hope such efforts will soon be forthcoming. In the interim we hope that this volume will help applied marketers (and academicians) to be more cautious in reviewing much of the BL research and findings published to date.

References

Anderson, Beverlee B. "Working Women Versus Non-Working Women: A Comparison of Shopping Behaviors." *Proceedings.* American Marketing Association, 1972, Pp. 355–359.

Anderson, Evan E. "The Measurement of Buyer Brand Preference and Indifference under Changing Terms of Trade." *American Journal of Agricultural Economics,* **56**, 122–128 (1974).

Aronson, Elliot and J. Merrill Carlsmith. "Experimentation in Social Psychology." In Gardner Lindzey and Elliot Aronson, Eds., *Handbook of Social Psychology,* Vol. 2. Reading, Massachusetts: Addison-Wesley, 1968.

Axelrod, Joel L. "Attitude Measures that Predict Purchase." *Journal of Advertising Research,* **8**, 3–17 (1968).

Bass, Frank M. "The Theory of Stochastic Preference and Brand Switching." *Journal of Marketing Research,* **11**, 1–20 (1974).

Bass, Frank M., Abel Jeuland, and Gordon P. Wright. "Equilibrium Stochastic Choice and Market Penetration Theory: Derivations and Comparisons." *Management Science,* **22** (10), 1051–1063 (1976).

Bass, Frank M. and Gordon P. Wright. "Some New Results in Purchase Timing and Brand Selection." Institute for Research in the Behavioral, Economic, and Management Sciences, Paper No. 583. Krannert Graduate School of Management, Purdue University, December 1976.

Becker, Gary S. "A Theory of the Allocation of Time." *The Economic Journal,* **75** (September), 493–517 (1965).

Bellenger, Danny N., Earle Steinberg, and Wilbur W. Stanton. "The Congruence of Store Image and Self Image: As It Relates to Store Loyalty." *Journal of Retailing,* **52** (1), 17–32 (1976).

Bettman, James R. *An Information Processing Theory of Consumer Choice*. Reading, Massachusetts: Addison-Wesley, in preparation.

Bettman, James R. and Jacob Jacoby. "Patterns of Processing in Consumer Information Acquisition." In Beverlee B. Anderson, Ed., *Advances in Consumer Research,* Vol. 3. Association for Consumer Research, 1976. Pp. 315–320.

Bennett, Peter D. and Harold H. Kassarjian. *Consumer Behavior*. Englewood Cliffs, New Jersey: Prentice-Hall, 1972. Pp. 40–43.

Bodi, Michael James. "Investigation of Sheth's Analytical Model of Brand Loyalty." *Dissertation Abstracts,* **32**, 4771-A (1972).

Bohrnstedt, George W. "Reliability and Validity Assessment in Attitude Measurement." In Gene F. Summers, Ed., *Attitude Measurement*. Chicago: Rand McNally, 1970. Pp. 80–99.

Bourne, Lyle E. *Human Conceptual Behavior*. Boston: Allyn & Bacon, 1966.

Bradley, R. A. and M. E. Terry. Rank Analysis of Incomplete Block Designs. I. The Analysis of Paired Comparisons. *Biometrika,* **39**, 1952. Pp. 324–325.

Braunstein, Myron L. *Depth Perception Through Motion*. New York: Academic Press, 1976.

Brown, George H. "Brand Loyalty—fact or fiction?" *Advertising Age,* **23**, 53–55 (June 19, 1952); **23**, 45–47 (June 30, 1952); **23**, 54–56 (July 14, 1952); **23**, 46–48 (July 28, 1952); **23**, 56–58 (August 11, 1952); **23**, 76–79 (September 1, 1952).

Brown, Joseph D. "Consumer Loyalty for Private Food Brands." Bureau of Business Research, Report No. 3. Muncie, Indiana: Ball State University, October 1972.

Bruner, Jerome S., Jacqueline J. Goodnow, and George A. Austin. *A Study of Thinking*. New York: Wiley, 1956.

Bubb, Peter Lawrence and David John van Rest. "Loyalty as a Component of the Industrial Buying Decision." *Industrial Marketing Management,* **3**, 25–32 (1973).

Burford, Roger L., Ben M. Enis, and Gordon W. Paul. "An Index for the Measurement of Consumer Loyalty." *Decision Sciences,* **2**, 17–24 (1971).

Byrne, Donn. *The Attraction Paradigm*. New York: Academic Press, 1971.

Byrne, Donn and W. Griffitt. "Interpersonal Attraction." In P. H. Mussen and M. R. Rosenzweig, Eds., *Annual Review of Psychology,* Vol. 24. 1973. Pp. 317–337.

Campbell, Donald T. and Donald W. Fiske. "Convergent and Discriminant Validation by the Multitrait-Multimethod Matrix." *Psychological Bulletin,* **56**, 81–105 (1959).

Campbell, John R. "Psychometric Theory." In Marvin D. Dunnette, Ed., *The Handbook of Industrial and Organizational Psychology.* Chicago: Rand McNally, 1976. Pp. 185–222.

Carman, James M. "Correlates of Brand Loyalty: Some Positive Results." *Journal of Marketing Research,* **7**, 67–76 (1970).

Carnap, Rudolf. *Logical Foundations of Probability.* Chicago: University of Chicago Press, 1950.

Chaplin, James P. and T. S. Krawiec. *Systems and Theories of Psychology.* New York: Holt, Rinehart & Winston, 1960.

Charlton, P. and Andrew S. C. Ehrenberg. "An Experiment in Brand Choice." *Journal of Marketing Research,* **13** (May), 152–160 (1976).

Chestnut, Robert W. "The Expenditure of Time in the Acquisition of Package Information," Unpublished master's thesis, Purdue University, 1975.

Chestnut, Robert W. "Information Acquisition in Life Insurance Policy Selection: Monitoring the Impact of Product Beliefs, Affect toward Agent, and External Memory." Unpublished doctoral dissertation, Purdue University, 1977.

Chestnut, Robert W. and Jacob Jacoby. "Consumer Information Processing: Emerging Theory and Findings." In Arch Woodside, Peter D. Bennett, and Jagdish N. Sheth, Eds., *Foundations of Consumer and Industrial Buyer Behavior.* New York: American Elsevier, 1977. Pp. 119–133.

Churchill, H. "How to Measure Brand Loyalty." *Advertising and Selling,* **35**, 24 (1942).

Cook, Thomas D. and Donald T. Campbell. "The Design and Conduct of Quasi-Experiments and True Experiments in Field Settings." In Marvin D. Dunnette, Ed., *The Handbook of Industrial and Organizational Psychology.* Chicago: Rand McNally, 1976. Pp. 223–326.

Copeland, Melvin T. "Relation of Consumer's Buying Habits to Marketing Methods." *Harvard Business Review,* **1** (April), 282–289 (1923).

Cronbach, Lee J. *Essentials of Psychological Testing,* 2nd ed. New York: Harper & Bros., 1960.

Cronbach, Lee J. and Paul E. Meehl. "Construct Validity in Psychological Tests." *Psychological Bulletin,* **52,** 281–302 (1955).

Cunningham, Ross M. "Brand Loyalty—What, Where, How Much?" *Harvard Business Review,* **34** (January-February), 116–128 (1956a).

Cunningham, Ross M. "Brand Loyalty—What, Where, How Much? *Journal of Marketing,* **21,** 206 (1956b).

Cunningham, Scott M. "Perceived Risk and Brand Loyalty." In D. Cox, Ed., *Risk Taking and Information Handling in Consumer Behavior.* Boston: Harvard University Press, 1967. Pp. 507–523.

Day, George S. "A Two-Dimensional Concept of Brand Loyalty." *Journal of Advertising Research,* **9,** 29–35 (1969).

Dommermuth, William P. "Shopping Matrix and Marketing Strategy." *Journal of Marketing Research,* **2**(2), 128–132 (1965).

Dupuy, George McVicar. "The Institutional Loyalty of New Residents: The Bank Selection Decision." *Dissertation Abstracts,* **35** (February), 4784A (1975).

Ehrenberg, Andrew S. C. "Estimating the Proportion of Loyal Buyers." *Journal of Marketing Research,* **1,** 56–59 (1964).

Ehrenberg, Andrew S. C. "Some Coherent Patterns." In Andrew S. C. Ehrenberg and F. G. Pyatt, Eds., *Consumer Behavior.* Baltimore: Penguin Books, 1971. Pp. 67–108.

Ehrenberg, Andrew S. C., Ed. *Repeat Buying: Theory and Applications.* New York: American Elsevier, 1972.

Ehrenberg, Andrew S. C. *Data Reduction and Interpreting Statistical Data.* New York: Wiley, 1975.

Ehrenberg, Andrew S. C. and G. J. Goodhardt. "A Comparison of American and British Repeat Buying Habits." *Journal of Marketing Research,* **5,** 29–33 (1968).

Engel, James E., David T. Kollat, and Roger D. Blackwell. *Consumer Behavior,* 1st ed. New York: Holt, Rinehart & Winston, 1968. Pp. 575–610.

Engel, James E., David T. Kollat, and Roger D. Blackwell. *Consumer Behavior,* 2nd ed. New York: Holt, Rinehart & Winston, 1973. Pp. 547–575.

Farley, John U. "Why Does Brand Loyalty Vary Over Products?" *Journal of Marketing Research,* **1,** 9–14 (1964a).

Farley, John U. "Brand Loyalty and the Economics of Information." *Journal of Business,* **37,** 370–381 (1964b).

Fishbein, Martin and Icek Ajzen. *Belief, Attitude, Intention and Behavior: An Introduction to Theory and Research.* Reading, Massachusetts: Addison-Wesley, 1975.

Fogg, C. Davis. "Planning Gains in Market Share." *Journal of Marketing,* **38** (3), 30–38 (1974).

Frank, Ronald E. "Brand Choice as Probability Process." *Journal of Business,* **35**, 43–56 (1962).

Frank, Ronald E., Susan P. Douglas, and Rolando Polli. "Household Correlates of Brand Loyalty for Grocery Products." *Journal of Business,* **41**, 237–245 (1968).

Fry, Joseph N., David C. Shaw, C. Haehling von Lanzenauer, and Cecil R. Dipchand. "Customer Loyalty to Banks: A Longitudinal Study." *The Journal of Business,* **46**, 517–525 (1973).

Gieselman, R. D. "Automobile Brand Loyalty." *Dissertation Abstracts,* **32**, 2670-A (1970).

Gruber, Alin. "Purchase Intent and Purchase Probability." *Journal of Advertising Research,* **10**, 23–27 (1970).

Guest, Lester P. "Last vs. Usual Purchase Questions." *Journal of Applied Psychology,* **26**, 180–186 (1942).

Guest, Lester P. "A Study of Brand Loyalty." *Journal of Applied Psychology,* **28**, 16–27 (1944).

Guest, Lester P. "Brand Loyalty—Twelve Years Later." *Journal of Applied Psychology,* **39**, 405–408 (1955).

Guest, Lester P. "Brand Loyalty Revisited: A Twenty Year Report." *Journal of Applied Psychology,* **48** (2), 93–97 (1964).

Guilford, Joy P. *Fundamental Statistics in Psychology and Education.* New York: McGraw-Hill, 1956.

Hall, Calvin S. and Gardner Lindzey. *Theories of Personality.* New York: Wiley, 1957.

Harary, Frank and Benjamin Lipstein. "The Dynamics of Brand Loyalty: A Markovian Approach." *Operations Research,* **10**, 19–40 (1962).

Hartigan, John A. *Clustering Algorithms.* New York: Wiley, 1975.

Heeler, Roger M. and Michael L. Ray. "Measure Validation in Marketing." *Journal of Marketing Research,* **9** (4), 361–370 (1972).

Herniter, Jerome D. "An Entropy Model of Brand Purchase Behavior." *Journal of Marketing Research,* **10**, 361–375 (1973).

Howard, John A. and Jagdish N. Sheth. *The Theory of Buyer Behavior.* New York: Wiley, 1969. Pp. 229–274.

Howard, John. *Consumer Behavior: An Application of Theory.* New York: McGraw-Hill, 1977.

Hughes, G. David. "Buyer/Consumer Information Processing: An Overview of Where Researchers Have Been and Where They Should Be Going." In. G. David Hughes and Michael L. Ray, Eds., *Buyer/Consumer Information Processing.* Chapel Hill, North Carolina: The University of North Carolina Press, 1974. Pp. 3–11.

Insko, Chester A. *Theories of Attitude Change.* New York: Appleton-Century-Crofts,1967.

Jacoby, Jacob. "Toward a Multi-Brand Model of Brand Loyalty." *Purdue Papers in Consumer Psychology.* Paper No. 105, 1969.

Jacoby, Jacob. "An Attitudinal Model of Multi-Brand Loyalty." Paper presented at the Spring Conference on Research Methodology. American Marketing Association, New York Chapter, New York City, May 1970.

Jacoby, Jacob. "Brand Loyalty: A Conceptual Definition." *Proceedings,* Vol. 6. American Psychological Association, 1971a. Pp. 655–656.

Jacoby, Jacob. "A Model of Multi-Brand Loyalty." *Journal of Advertising Research,* 11, 25–30 (1971b).

Jacoby, Jacob. "A Brand Loyalty Concept: Comments on a Comment." *Journal of Marketing Research,* 12 (3), 484–487 (1975).

Jacoby, Jacob, Carol K. Berning, and Thomas F. Dietvorst. "What about Disposition?" *Journal of Marketing,* 41, No. 2, April, 22–28 (1977).

Jacoby, Jacob, Robert W. Chestnut, and William Fisher. "Simulating Non-Durable Purchase: Individual Differences and Information Acquisition Behavior." Accepted, *Journal of Marketing Research,* 1977a.

Jacoby, Jacob and Robert W. Chestnut. "Amount, Type, and Order of Package Information Acquisition in Purchasing Decisions." Final report submitted to the National Science Foundation, RANN (GI-43687), 1977b.

Jacoby, Jacob and Robert W. Chestnut. *Human Problem Solving: A Behavioral Process Approach.* In preparation.

Jacoby, Jacob, Robert W. Chestnut, Karl C. Weigl, and William Fisher. "Pre-Purchase Information Acquisition: Description of a Process Methodology, Research Paradigm, and Pilot Investigation." In Beverlee B. Anderson, Ed., *Advances in Consumer Research*, Vol. 3. Association for Consumer Research, 1976. Pp. 306–314.

Jacoby, Jacob, Wesley Jones, and Robert W. Chestnut. "Intent to Purchase and the Regions of Brand Acceptance." *Purdue Papers in Consumer Psychology*, in preparation.

Jacoby, Jacob and David B. Kyner. "Brand Loyalty vs. Repeat Purchasing Behavior." *Journal of Marketing Research*, **10**, 1–9 (1973).

Jacoby, Jacob and Jerry C. Olson. "An Attitudinal Model of Brand Loyalty: Conceptual Underpinnings and Instrumentation Research." Paper presented at the University of Illinois Conference on Attitude Research and Consumer Behavior. Urbana, Illinois, December 1970. (Available as Purdue Papers in Consumer Psychology, No. 159.)

Jacoby, Jacob and Jerry C. Olson. "Consumer Reaction to Price: An Attitudinal, Information-Processing Perspective. In Yoram Wind and Marvin Greenberg, Eds., *Moving Ahead with Attitude Research*. Chicago: American Marketing Association, 1977, Pp. 73–86.

Jacoby, Jacob, Jerry C. Olson, and George J. Szybillo. "Operationalizing an Attitudinal Model of Multi-Brand Loyalty: Second Report." A proprietary report to the Pillsbury Company. April 1971.

Jacoby, Jacob, George J. Szybillo, and Jacqueline Busato-Schach. "Information Acquisition Behavior in Brand Choice Situations." *Journal of Consumer Research*, **3**, 209–216 (1977).

Jarvis, Lance P. and James B. Wilcox. "Repeat Purchasing Behavior and Attitudinal Brand Loyalty: Additional Evidence." In Kenneth L. Bernhardt, Ed., *Marketing: 1776–1976 and Beyond*. American Marketing Association, 1976. Pp. 151–152.

Jenkins, John G. "Dependability of Psychological Brand Barometers: I. The Problem of Reliability." *Journal of Applied Psychology*, **22**, 1–7 (1938).

Juster, F. Thomas. "Consumer Buying Intentions and Purchase Probability, an Experiment in Survey Design." National Bureau of Economic Research, Occasional Paper 99. New York: Columbia University Press, 1966.

Kaplan, Abraham. *The Conduct of Inquiry*. San Francisco: Chandler Publications, 1964.

Kerlinger, Fred N. *Foundations of Behavioral Research*. New York: Holt, Rinehart & Winston, 1964.

Kiesler, Charles A. "Commitment." In Robert P. Abelson, Elliot Aronson, William J. McGuire, Milton J. Rosenberg, Theodore M. Newcomb, and Percy H. Tannenbaum, Eds., *Theories of Cognitive Consistency: A Sourcebook*. Skokie, Illinois: Rand McNally, 1968. Pp. 448–455.

Kiesler, Charles A. *The Psychology of Commitment*. New York: Academic Press, 1971.

Kiesler, Charles A., Barry E. Collins, and Norman Miller. *Attitude Change*. New York: Wiley, 1969.

Kuehn, Alfred A. "An Analysis of the Dynamics of Consumer Behavior and Its Implications of Marketing Management." Unpublished doctoral dissertation. Pittsburgh: Carnegie Institute of Technology, 1958.

Kuehn, Alfred A. "Demonstration of a Relationship between Psychological Factors and Brand Choice." *Journal of Business*, **36**, 237–241 (1963).

Kuehn, Alfred A. and Ralph L. Day. "A Probabilistic Approach to Consumer Behavior." In Reavis Cox, Ed., *Theory in Marketing*. Homewood, Illinois: Irwin, 1964.

Lamont, Lawrence M. and James T. Rothe. "The Impact of Unit Pricing on Channel Systems." *Proceedings*. American Marketing Association, 1971. Pp. 653–658.

Linder, S. B. *The Harried Leisure Class*. New York: Columbia University Press, 1970.

Link, Henry C. "A New Method for Testing Advertising and a Psychological Sales Barometer." *Journal of Applied Psychology*, **18**, 1–26 (1934).

Lipstein, Benjamin. "The Dynamics of Brand Loyalty and Brand Switching." *Proceedings*. Fifth Annual Conference of the Advertising Research Foundation, New York, 1959.

Livesy, Frank. "Brand Loyalty and the Television Rental Market." *European Journal of Marketing*, **7** (3), 218–231 (1973/74).

Lutz, Richard J. and Paul R. Winn. "Developing a Bayesian Measure of Brand Loyalty: A Preliminary Report." In R. C. Corhan, Ed., *1974 Combined Proceedings*. Chicago: American Marketing Association, 1975. Pp. 104–108.

McCann, John M. "Market Segment Response to the Marketing De-

REFERENCES

cision Variables." *Journal of Marketing Research,* **11,** 399–412 (1974).

McConnell, J. Douglas. "The Development of Brand Loyalty: An Empirical Study." *Journal of Marketing Research,* **5,** 13–19 (1968a).

McConnell, J. Douglas. "The Effect of Pricing in an Experimental Setting." *Journal of Applied Psychology,* **52,** 331–334 (1968b).

McGregor, Douglas. "'Motives' as a Tool of Market Research." *Harvard Business Review,* **29,** 42–51 (1940).

McGuire, William J. "The Nature of Attitudes and Attitude Change." In Gardner Lindzey and Elliot Aronson, Eds., *The Handbook of Social Psychology,* Vol. 3, 2nd ed. Reading, Massachusetts: Addison-Wesley, 1969. Pp. 136–314.

McGuire, William J. "Some Internal Psychological Factors Influencing Consumer Choice." *Journal of Consumer Research,* **2,** 302–319 (1976).

McHale, Henry Patrick. "Correlates of Brand Loyalty in the Automobile Industry." *Dissertation Abstracts,* 31, 6221-A (1971).

Massaro, Dominic W. *Experimental Psychology and Information Processing.* Chicago: Rand McNally, 1975.

Massy, William F. "Brand and Store Loyalty as Bases for Market Segmentation." In J. Newman, Ed., *On Knowing the Consumer.* New York: John Wiley and Sons, 1966. Pp. 169–172.

Massy, William F., Ronald E. Frank, and Thomas M. Lodahl. *Purchasing Behavior and Personal Attributes.* Philadelphia: University of Pennsylvania Press, 1968.

MIT Report: Consumer Appliances—The Real Cost. A study conducted by the MIT Center for Policy Alternatives and the Charles Stark Draper Laboratory, Inc. Washington, D.C.: National Science Foundation (RANN Documentation Center), 1974.

Mitchell, Andrew A. and Jerry C. Olson. "The Use of Restricted and Unrestricted Maximum Likelihood Factor Analysis to Examine Alternative Measures of Brand Loyalty." Pennsylvania State University, *Working Series in Marketing Research,* No. 38, 1975.

Monroe, Kent B. and Joseph P. Guiltinan. "A Path-Analytic Exploration of Retail Patronage Influences." *Journal of Consumer Research,* **2,** 19–28 (1975).

Newman, Joseph W. and Richard A. Werbel. "Multivariate Analysis of Brand Loyalty for Major Household Appliances." *Journal of Marketing Research*, **10**, 404–409 (1973).

Nicosia, Franco M. *Consumer Decision Processes: Marketing and Advertising Implications*. Englewood Cliffs, New Jersey: Prentice-Hall, 1966.

Nordstrom, Richard D. and John E. Swan. "Does a Change in Customer Loyalty Occur When a New Car Agency is Sold?" *Journal of Marketing Research*, **13**, 173–177 (1976).

Nunnally, Jum C. *Psychometric Theory*. New York: McGraw-Hill, 1967.

Nunnally, Jum C. *Introduction to Psychological Measurement*. New York: McGraw-Hill, 1970.

Olson, Jerry C. and Jacob Jacoby. "A Construct Validation Study of Brand Loyalty." *Proceedings* Vol. 6. American Psychological Association, 1971. Pp. 657–658.

Olson, Jerry C. and Jacob Jacoby. "Cue Utilization in the Quality Perception Process." In M. Venkatesan, Ed., *Proceedings*, Vol. 2. The Association for Consumer Research, 1972. Pp. 167–179.

Olson, Jerry C. and Jacob Jacoby. "Measurement of Multi-Brand Loyalty." Paper presented at the Brand Loyalty Symposium, Fourth Annual Conference of the Association for Consumer Research. Boston, November 1973.

Olson, Jerry C. and Aydin Muderrisoglu. "Bibliography of Selected References on Cognitive and Information Processing Phenomena." Unpublished working paper, The Pennsylvania State University, March, 1977.

Payne, John W. "Heuristic Search Processes in Decision Making." In Beverlee B. Anderson, Ed., *Advances in Consumer Research*, Vol. 3. Association for Consumer Research, 1976. Pp. 321–327.

Pessemier, Edgar A. "A New Way to Determine Buying Decisions." *Journal of Marketing*, **24**, 41–46 (1959)

Plutchik, Robert. *Foundations of Experimental Research*. New York: Harper and Row, 1968.

Posner, Michael I. *Cognition: An Introduction*. Glenview, Illinois: Scott, Foresman, 1973.

Psychological Review, Vol. 52. American Psychological Association, 1945. Pp. 241–294.

Reynolds, Fred D., William R. Darden, and Warren S. Martin. "Developing an Image of the Store-Loyal Customer: A Life-

Style Analysis to Probe a Neglected Market." *Journal of Retailing,* **50** (4), 73–84 (1974/1975).

Reynolds, Fred D. and William D. Wells. *Consumer Behavior.* New York: McGraw-Hill, 1977.

Rice, W. "Measurement of Consumer Loyalty: Factor Analysis as a Market Research Tool." Unpublished master's thesis. Cambridge. Massachusetts: MIT, 1962.

Seggev, Eli. "Brand Assortment and Consumer Brand Choice." *Journal of Marketing,* **34,** 18–24 (1970).

Selltiz, Claire, Marie Jahoda, Morton Deutsch, and Stuart W. Cook. *Research Methods in Social Relations,* rev. ed. New York: Henry Holt & Co., 1960.

Shapiro, Benson P. "The Effect of Price on Purchase Behavior." In David L. Sparks, Ed., *AMA Fall Educators Conference.* Chicago: American Marketing Association, 1970.

Sherif, Carolyn and Carl I. Hovland. *Social Judgment: Assimilation and Contrast Effects in Communication and Attitude Change.* New Haven, Connecticut: Yale University Press, 1961.

Sherif, Carolyn W., Muzafer Sherif, and R. Nebergall. *Attitude and Attitude Change.* Philadelphia: W. B. Saunders Co., 1965.

Sherif, Muzafer and Carolyn W. Sherif. *Attitude, Ego Involvement and Change.* New York: Wiley, 1967.

Sheth, Jagdish N. "A Factor Analytic Model of Brand Loyalty." *Journal of Marketing Research,* **5,** 395–404 (1968).

Sheth, Jagdish N. "Measurement of Multidimensional Brand Loyalty." *Journal of Marketing Research,* **7,** 348–354 (1970).

Sheth, Jagdish N. and Whan C. Park. "A Theory of Multi-Dimensional Brand Loyalty." *Proceedings.* Association for Consumer Research, 1974. Pp. 449–459.

Speller, Donald E. "Attitudes and Intentions as Predictors of Purchase: A Cross-Validation." *Proceedings,* Vol. 8. American Psychological Association, 1973. Pp. 825–826.

Szybillo, George J. and Jacob Jacoby. "Intrinsic vs. Extrinsic Cues as Determinants of Perceived Product Quality." *Journal of Applied Psychology,* **59** (1), 74–78 (1974).

Tarpey, Lawrence X., Sr. "A Brand Loyalty Concept—A Comment." *Journal of Marketing Research,* **11** (2), 214–217 (1974).

Tarpey, Lawrence X., Sr. "Brand Loyalty Revisited: A Commentary." *Journal of Marketing Research,* **12** (November), 488–491 (1975).

Torgerson, Warren S. *Theory and Methods of Scaling*. New York: John Wiley and Sons, 1958.

Towle, Jeffrey G. and Claude R. Martin, Jr. "The Elderly Consumer: One Segment or Many?" In Beverlee B. Anderson, Ed., *Advances in Consumer Research*, Vol. 3. Association for Consumer Research, 1976. Pp. 463–468.

Tucker, W. T. "The Development of Brand Loyalty." *Journal of Marketing Research*, **1**, 32–35 (1964).

Wind, Yoram. "Industrial Source Loyalty." *Journal of Marketing Research*, **7**, 450–457 (1970).

Wind, Yoram. "Brand Choice." In Robert Ferber, Ed., *Synthesis of Knowledge on Consumer Behavior*. National Science Foundation (RANN) Project, 1975.

Winters, Frederick W. "Laboratory Measurement of Response to Consumer Information." *Journal of Marketing Research*, **12** (4), 390–401 (1975).

Woodside, Arch G. and James D. Clokey. "A General Model of Consumer Brand Switching Behavior." In Edward M. Mazze, Ed., *1975 Combined Proceedings*. American Marketing Association, 1975, Pp. 175–180.

Wright, Peter. "The Harassed Decision Maker: Time Pressure, Distractions, and the Use of Evidence." *Journal of Applied Psychology*, **59** (5), 555–561 (1974).

Wright, Peter and Fredrick Barbour. "Phased Decision Strategies: Sequels to an Initial Screening." Stanford University, *Research Paper Series*, No. 353, 1977.

Supplemental References

Aaker, D. A. "A New Method for Evaluating Stochastic Models of Brand Choice." *Journal of Marketing Research,* **7,** 300–306 (1970).

Aaker, D. A. "The New-trier Stochastic Model of Brand Choice." *Management Science,* **17,** B435–450 (1971a).

Aaker, D. A. and Jones, J. M. "Modeling Store Choice Behavior." *Journal of Marketing Research,* **8,** 38–42 (1971b).

Aaker, D. A. "A Measure of Brand Acceptance." *Journal of Marketing Research,* **9,** 160–167 (1972).

Alemson, M. A. and Burley, H. T. "Demand and Entry into an Oligopolistic Market: A Case Study." *The Journal of Industrial Economics,* **23,** 109–117 (1974).

Allen, C. L. "How Often and What People Buy." *Journal of Marketing,* **14,** 609 (1950).

Allison, R. I. and Uhl, K. P. "Influence of Beer Brand Identification on Taste Perception." *Journal of Marketing Research,* **5,** 36–39 (1964).

Anderson, L. K., Taylor, J. R., and Holloway, R. J. "The Consumer and His Alternatives: An Experimental Approach." *Journal of Marketing Research,* **3,** 62–67 (1966).

Anon. "Family Buying Decisions: Who Makes Them, Who Influences Them?" *Printers Ink,* **264,** 21–29 (1958).

Anon. "Closed Set of Brands Explained to ARF: Its Statistical Perpetual Motion." *Advertising Age,* **30,** 1 (1959).

Arndt, J. "Word of Mouth Advertising and Perceived Risk." In H. H. Kassarjian and T. S. Robertson, (Eds.), *Perspectives in Consumer Behavior*. Glenview, Illinois: Scott, 1968. Pp. 330–336.

Banks, S. "The Relationships Between Preference and Purchase of Brands." *Journal of Marketing*, 15, 145–157 (1950).

Banks, S. "Some Correlates of Coffee and Cleanser Brand Shares." *Journal of Advertising Research*, 1, 22–28 (1960).

Barclay, W. D. "The Semantic Differential as an Index of Brand Attitude." *Journal of Advertising Research*, 4, 30–33 (1964).

Barnet, E. M. "Showdown in the Market Place." *Harvard Business Review*, 34, 85–96 (1956).

Barton, S. G. "The Movement of Branded Goods and the Consumer." In A. S. Blankenship, (Ed.), *How to Conduct Consumer and Opinion Research*. New York: Harper, 1946. Pp. 58–70.

Bass, F. M., Pessemier, E. A., and Tigert, D. J. "Complementary and Substitute Patterns of Purchasing and Use." *Journal of Advertising Research*, 9, 19–29 (1969).

Bauer, R. "Negroes More Brand Conscious Than Whites." *Advertising Age*, 35(12), 73 (1964).

Baum, J. and Dennis, K. E. R. "The Estimation of the Expected Brand Share of a New Product." *Esomar Congress*, Baden-Baden, 1961.

Benson, P. H. "Individual Exposure to Advertising and Changes in Brands Bought." *Journal of Advertising Research*, 7, 27–31 (1967).

Bird, M., Charmon, C., and Ehrenberg, A. S. C. "Brand Image and Brand Usage." *Journal of Marketing Research*, 7, 307–314 (1970).

Bird, M. and Ehrenberg, A. S. C. "Intentions-to-Buy and Claimed Brand Usage." *Operations Research Quarterly*, 17, 27–46 (1966).

Blackwell, R. D., Engel, J. F., and Kollat, D. T., (Eds.), *Cases in Consumer Behavior*. New York: Holt, Reinhart, & Winston, 1969. Pp. 298–314.

Blattberg, Robert C. and Sen, S. K. "A Bayesian Technique to Discriminate Between Stochastic Models of Brand Choice." *Management Science*, 21, 682–696 (1975).

Blattberg, Robert C. and Sen, S. K. "Market Segmentation Using Models of Multidimensional Purchasing Behavior." *Journal of Marketing,* **38,** 17–28 (1974).

Blattberg, Robert C. and Sen, S. K. "Market Segments and Stochastic Brand Choice Models." *Journal of Marketing Research,* **13,** 34–45 (1976).

Blattberg, Robert C., Peacock, P., and Sen, S. K. "Modeling Brand Choice Strategies Across Product Categories." In K. L. Bernhardt, Ed., *Marketing: 1776–1976 and Beyond.* Chicago: American Marketing Association, 1976.

Boedecker, K. A. "The Impact of Advertising Themes on Brand Choice of Color Television Sets: An Exploratory Survey of the Lansing Major Metropolitan Market." *Dissertation Abstracts,* **36,** 387-A (1975).

Brody, R. P. and Cunningham, S. M. "Personality Variables and the Consumer Decision Process." *Journal of Marketing Research,* **5,** 50–57 (1968).

Brooks, C. "Relating the Selling Effort to Patterns of Purchase Behavior." *Journal of Marketing,* **27,** 94 (1963).

Brown, G. H. "Less Than 15 Percent of Chicago Margarine Users Are Loyal to One Brand; Half Buy Four or More Brands. Almost Half of Chicago Toothpaste Users Are Loyal to One Brand; Contrasts with Margarine Buying." *Journal of Marketing,* **17,** 193 (1952).

Brown, G. H. "Brown Clarifies Share-of-Market Figures in Brand Loyalty." *Journal of Marketing,* **17,** 304 (1953).

Brown, W. F. "The Determination of Factors Influencing Brand Choice." *Journal of Marketing,* **19,** 699–706 (1950).

Brunner, C. E. "An Exploration of the Relationship Between Product, Brand, and Shopping Involvement and Brand Alternative Consideration." *Dissertation Abstracts,* **34,** 5387-A (1974).

Campbell, B. M. "The Existence of Evoked Set and Determinants of Its Magnitude in Brand Choice Behavior." Unpublished doctoral dissertation. New York: Columbia University, 1969.

Caplan, M. "A Measure of the Effect of Special Price Inducements on Loyalty Behavior." B. S. thesis. Cambridge, Massachusetts: School of Industrial Management, MIT, June 1954.

Carman, J. M. "Brand Switching and Linear Learning Models." *Journal of Advertising Research,* **6,** 23–31 (1966).

Carman, J. M. "Some Insights Into Reasonable Grocery Shopping Strategies." *Journal of Marketing,* **33,** 69–72 (1969).

Chance, W. A. and French, N. A. "An Exploratory Investigation of Brand Switching." *Journal of Marketing Research,* **9,** 226–229 (1972).

Charlton, P., Ehrenberg, A. S. C., and Pymont, B. "Buyer Behavior Under Mini-test Conditions." *Journal of the Market Research Society,* **14,** 171–183 (1972).

Charlton, P. "A Review of Shop Loyalty." *Journal of the Market Research Society,* **15,** 35–51 (1973).

Charlton, P. and Ehrenberg, A. S. C. "McConnell's Experimental Brand Choice Data." *Journal of Marketing Research,* **10,** 302–307 (1973).

Chestnut, R. W. and Weigl, K. "A Shopping-prone Scale." *Purdue Papers in Consumer Psychology,* in preparation.

Clarke, D. G. "Cumulative Advertising Effects: Sources and Implications." *Marketing Science Institute,* Report No. 77-111, 1977.

Clausen, E. A. "Marketing Ethics and the Consumer." *Harvard Business Review,* (January and February), (1967), pp. 79–86.

Claycamp, H. J. and Liddy, L. E. "Prediction of New Brand Performance: An Analytical Approach." *Journal of Marketing Research,* **6,** 414–420 (1969).

Coffin, T. "Study Shows Buyers Brand Choice Definitely Influenced by Ads." *Advertising Age,* **34,** 38 (January 14, 1963).

Cohen, J. B. and Goldberg, M. E. "The Dissonance Model in Post-decision Product Evaluation." *Journal of Marketing Research,* **7,** 315–321 (1970).

Cohen, J. B. and Houston, M. J. "Cognitive Consequences of Brand Loyalty." *Journal of Marketing Research,* **9,** 97–99 (1972).

Comish, N. H. "Why Customers Change Brands." *Journal of Marketing,* **18,** 66 (1953).

Coulson, J. S. "Buying Decisions Within the Family and the Consumer-brand Relationship." In Newman, (Ed.), *On Knowing the Consumer.* New York: Wiley, 1966. Pp. 59–66.

Cox, K. K., (Ed.) *Marketing Research: Addresses, Essays, Lectures.* New York: Appleton-Century-Crofts, 1967.

Cummings, W. H. and Venkatesan, M. "Cognitive Dissonance and Consumer Behavior: A Critical Review." *Working Paper Series No. 74-1,* The University of Iowa, January 1974. Pp. 59–66.

Cunningham, M. T. and Kettlewood, K. "Source Loyalty in the Freight Transport Market." *European Journal of Marketing,* **10,** 60–79 (1976).

Cunningham, R. M. "Measurement of Brand Loyalty." *The Marketing Revolution,* Proceedings of the thirty-seventh conference of the American Marketing Association. Chicago: American Marketing Association, 1956. Pp. 39–45.

Cunningham, R. M. "Customer Loyalty to Store and Brand." *Harvard Business Review,* **39,** 127–137 (November-December 1961).

Cunningham, R. M. "Buying Decisions Within the Family." In J. Newman, (Ed.), *On Knowing the Consumer.* New York: Wiley, 1966. Pp. 59–66.

Day, G. S. "Buyer Attitudes and Brand Choice Behavior." *Dissertation Abstracts,* **28,** 4658–4659 (1969).

DeBruicker, F. S. "Perceived Product Benefits, Stated Brand Preferences and Attitude and Activity Measures as Alternative Strategies for Market Segmentation." Unpublished doctoral dissertation, Purdue University, 1973.

Demsetz, H. "The Effect of Consumer Experience on Brand Loyalty and the Structure of Market Demand." *Econometrica,* **30,** 22–23 (1962).

Dewey, G. "How Advertising Influences Brand Preference of Machine Tool Buyers." *Journal of Marketing,* **26,** 100 (1962).

Dichter, E. "The World Customer." *Harvard Business Review,* (July and August), 1962, pp. 113–122.

Dodson, J. A., Tybout, A. M. and Sternthal, B. "The Impact of Deals and Deal Retraction on Brand Switching." To appear in *Journal of Marketing Research.* February 1978.

Donnahue, A. S. "Research Study of Consumer Loyalty." *Journal of Retailing,* **32,** 14–16 (1956).

Dorlich, I. J. "Congruence Relationships Between Self-images and product brands." *Journal of Marketing Research,* **6,** 80–84 (1969).

Draper, J. E. and Nolin, L. H. "A Markov Chain Analysis of Brand Preferences." *Journal of Advertising Research,* **4,** 50–55 (1964).

Eberhard, W. "Brand Policy Without Price Maintenance." *Journal of Marketing,* **27,** 107 (1963).

Ehrenberg, A. S. C. "The pattern of Consumer Purchases." *Applied Statistics,* **8,** 26–41 (1959).

Ehrenberg, A. S. C. "Verified Predictions of Consumer Purchasing Patterns." *Commentary*, **10**, 16–21 (1963).

Ehrenberg, A. S. C. "An Appraisal of Markov Brand Switching Models." *Journal of Marketing Research*, **2**, 347–362 (1965).

Ehrenberg, A. S. C. "The Practical Meaning and Usefulness of the NBD/LSD theory of Repeat Buying." *Applied Statistics*, **1**, 17–32 (1968).

Ehrenberg, A. S. C. "Towards an Integrated Theory of Consumer Behavior." *Journal of the Marketing Research Society*, **11**, 305–337 (1969).

Ehrenberg, A. S. C. "Loyalty Reports—A New Analysis Service." *Admap*, **5**, 162–164 (1969).

Ehrenberg, A. S. C. "Repeat Buying of New Brand: A 10 Point Case History." *Journal of Marketing*, **33**, 80 (1969).

Ehrenberg, A. S. C. "Loyalty Reports—A Coded Example." An unpublished paper, Aske Research Inc., New York, 1970.

Ehrenberg, A. S. C. and Goodhardt, G. J. "A Model of Multi-brand Buying." *Journal of Marketing Research*, **7**, 77–84 (1970).

Ehrenberg, A. S. C. and Charlton, P. "An Analysis of Simulated Brand Choice." *Journal of Advertising Research*, **13**, 21–33 (1973).

Emanuel, H. and Kloassen, L. "On the Interaction of Purchasing Motives and the Optimal Programming of Their Activation." *Journal of Marketing*, **25**, 88 (1961).

Empey, P. H. "A Stochastic Revealed Preference Approach to the Empirical Investigation of the Axiom of Consumer Consistency." Unpublished doctoral dissertation, Purdue University, 1972.

Engel, J. E. and Starn, L. W. "The Influence of Brand Preference on the Perception of Brand Names." *Journal of Marketing Research*, (Winter), (1964), pp. 197–211.

Engel, J. E., Wales, H. G., Warshaw, M. R., (Eds.) *Promotional Strategy*. Homewood, Illinois: 1967. Pp. 69–75.

Enis, B. M. and Paul, G. W. "Store Loyalty as a Basis for Market Segmentation." *Journal of Retailing*, **46**, 42–56 (1970).

Farley, J. U. "Testing a Theory of Brand Loyalty." In S. Greyser, (Ed.), *Toward Scientific Marketing*. Chicago: AMA, 1963. Pp. 308–315.

Farley, J. U. "A Test of the Brand Loyalty Proneness Hypothesis." *Commentary*, **8**, 35–42 (1966).

Farley, J. U. and Kuehn, A. A. "Stochastic Models of Brand Switching." In G. Schwartz, (Ed.), *Science in Marketing*. New York: Wiley 1965. Pp. 446–464.

Fleishman, E. A. "An Experimental Consumer Panel Technique." *Journal of Applied Psychology*, **35**, 133–135 (1951).

Fourt, L. A. and Woodlock, J. W. "Early Prediction of Market Success for New Grocery Products." *Journal of Marketing*, **25**, 31–38 (1960).

Frank, R. E. "Correlations of Buying Behavior for Grocery Products." *Journal of Marketing*, **31**, 48–54 (1967).

Frank, R. E. "Is Brand Loyalty a Useful Basis for Market Segmentation?" *Journal of Advertising Research*, **7**, 27–33 (1967).

Frank, R. E. and Boyd, H. W. "Are Private-brand-prone Grocery Customers Really Different?" *Journal of Advertising Research*, **5**, 27–35 (1965).

Frank, R. E. and Massy, W. R. "Innovation and Brand Choice: The Folger's Invasion." In S. Greyser, (Ed.), *Toward Scientific Marketing*. Chicago: AMA, 1963. Pp. 96–107.

Frank, R. E. and Massy, W. F. "Market Segmentation and the Effectiveness of a Brand's Price and Dealing Policies." *Journal of Business*, **38**, 186–200 (April 1965).

Frank, R. E., Massy, W. F., and Lodahl, T. M. "Purchasing Behavior and Personal Attributes." *Journal of Advertising Research*, **9**, 15–24 (1969).

Frank, R. E., Massy, W. F., and Morrison, D. G. "The Determinants of Innovative Behavior with Respect to a Branded Frequently Purchased Food Product." In G. L. Smith, (Ed.), *Reflections on Progress in Marketing*. AMA Proceedings, 1964. Pp. 312–323.

Freiberg, A. D. "Why People Buy a Certain Brand of Coffee." *Journal of Marketing*, **15**, 84 (1950).

Frevert, R. F. "An Observational Criterion of Repurchase Performance." *Journal of Marketing Research*, **4**, 249–251 (1967).

Fromkin, H. L. "A Social Psychological Analysis of the Adoption and Diffusion of New Products and Practices From a Uniqueness Motivation Perspective." *Proceedings*, 2nd Annual Conference, Association for Consumer Research, 1971. Pp. 464–469.

Fry, J. N. "Family Branding and Consumer Brand Choice." *Journal of Marketing Research*, **4**, 234–247 (1967).

Gardner, B. B. and Sidney, J. L. "The Product and the Brand." *Journal of Marketing*, **20**, 290 (1956).

Garlington, W. K. and Shimota, H. E. "The Change Seeker Index: A Measure of the Need for Variable Stimulus Input." *Psychological Reports,* **14,** 919–924 (1964).

Gates, W. "Multiple Product Grants and the Race for Diversification." *Magazine of Wall Street,* **90,** 8–10 (April 1952).

Gausel, A. "Determinants of Consumer Brand Switching: An Experiment." Unpublished doctoral dissertation, Harvard University, 1970.

Goodman, W. D. "Has the Private Brand Situation Changed?" *Canadian Tax Journal,* **12,** 275–280 (July, August 1964).

Grahn, G. L. "NBD Model of Repeat Purchase Loyalty: An Empirical Investigation." *Journal of Marketing Research,* **6,** 72–78 (1969).

Green, H. E. "You Can't Buy Brand Loyalty with Deals." *Journal of Marketing,* **17,** 303 (1953).

Greenberg, A. "Validity of a Brand Awareness Question." *Journal of Marketing,* **23,** 182–184 (October 1958).

Greene, J. D. and Stock, J. S. "Brand Attitudes as Measures of Advertising Effects." *Journal of Advertising Research,* **6,** 14–22 (1966).

Grilt, S. H., (Ed.) *Consumer Behavior and the Behavioral Sciences.* New York: Wiley, 1967.

Grit Publishing Co. "Small Towners Loyal to Brands." *Advertising Age,* **32,** 60 (December 11, 1961).

Grubb, E. L. and Hupp, G. "Perception of Self, Generalized Stereotypes, and Brand Selection." *Journal of Marketing Research,* **5,** 58–63 (1968).

Guest, L. P. "The Genesis of Brand Awareness." *The Journal of Applied Psychology,* **26,** 800–808 (1942).

Guest, L. "Brand Loyalty—Twelve Years Later." *Journal of Marketing,* **20,** 421 (1956).

Guetta, P. "Les Stéréotypes des Marques Commerciales et Leur Maniement." *Revue Psychologie Applique,* **9,** 1–9 (1959).

Hallaq, J. H. "An Analysis of the Development of Original Brand Loyalty for Nondurable Consumer Products." *Dissertation Abstracts,* **33,** 6517–A.

Harary, F. "Graph Theoretic Methods in the Management Sciences." *Management Science,* **5,** 387–403 (1959).

Haynes, P. "Consumer Loyalty and the Fugitive Market." *Canadian Packaging,* **14,** 37–42 (1961).

Herniter, J. D. and Howard, R. "Stochastic Marketing Models." In G. B. Hertz and R. T. Eddison, (Eds.), *Progress in Operations Research.* New York: Wiley, 1964.

Herniter, J. D. and Magee, J. F. "Customer Behavior as a Markov Process." *Operations Research,* **9**, 105–122 (1961).

Howard, R. A., (Ed.) *Dynamic Programming and Markov Processes.* New York: The Technology Press, MIT, and Wiley, 1960.

Howard, R. A. "Stochastic Process Models of Consumer Behavior— A Critical Review." Report of the 8th Meeting of the ARF Operations Research Discussion Group." November 21, 1962, New York, pp. 15–34.

Howard, R. A. "Stochastic Process Models of Consumer Behavior." *Journal of Advertising Research,* **3**, 35–42 (1963).

Howard, R. A. "Dynamic Inference." *Operations Research,* **13**, 712–733 (1965).

Ingram, M. V. "A Study of Negro-white Brand Loyalty." *Dissertation Abstracts,* **32**, 6608–A (1972).

Jacoby, J., Olson, J. C., and Kaplan, L. B. "Operationalizing an Attitudinal Model of Multi-brand Loyalty. Preliminary Results and Proposed Directions." A Proprietary Report to the Pillsbury Company, August 1970.

Jarvis, L. P. "An Empirical Investigation of Cognitive Brand Loyalty and Product Class Importance as Mediators of Consumer Brand Choice Behavior." *Dissertation Abstracts,* **34**, 943–A (1973).

Jephcott, J. "Consumer Loyalty—A Fresh Look." Paper read at the Market Research Society Conference, Brighton, England, 1972.

Jones, J. M. "A Comparison of Three Models of Brand Choice." *Journal of Marketing Research,* **7**, 466–473 (1970).

Jones, J. M. "A Dual-effects Model of Brand Choice." *Journal of Marketing Research,* **7**, 458–465 (1970).

Joyce, T. "Advertising's Major Role? Bolstering Brand Loyalty." *Advertising Age,* **69**, (May 1967).

Kanungo, R. N. "Brand Awareness: Differential Roles of Fittingness and Meaningfulness of Brand Names." *Journal of Applied Psychology,* **52**, 140–146 (1969).

Kanungo, R. N. and Dutta, S. "Brand Awareness as a Function of its Meaningfulness, Sequential Position, and Product Utility." *Journal of Applied Psychology,* **50**, 220–224 (1966).

Keming, J. and Snell, J. L., (Ed.) *Finite Markov Chains.* Princeton, New Jersey: Van Nostrand, 1960.

Kirsch, A. D., Berger, P. K., and Belfor, R. J. "Are Reports of Brand Bought Last Reliable and Valid? *Journal of Advertising Research,* **2,** 34–36 (1962).

Knopp, J. "Branding and the Robinson-Patman Act." *Journal of Business,* **39,** 24–34 (January 1966).

Kotler, P. "Operations Research in Marketing." *Harvard Business Review,* January-February 1967, pp. 31–33.

Kraft, F. B., Granbois, D. H., and Summers, J. O. "Brand Evaluation and Choice: A Longitudinal Study." *Journal of Marketing Research,* **10,** 235–241 (1973).

Krugman, H. E. "The Learning of Consumer Preference." *Journal of Marketing,* **26,** 31–35 (1962).

Krugman, H. E. "Comments on Patterns of Buyer Behavior." *Journal of Marketing Research,* **7,** 120 (1970).

Kuehn, A. A. "Consumer Brand Choice as a Learning Process." *Journal of Advertising Research,* **2,** 10–17 (1962).

Kuehn, A. A. "Consumer Brand Choice—a Learning Process?" In Frank, Kuehn, and Massy, Eds., *Quantitative Techniques in Marketing Analysis.* Homewood, Illinois: Irwin, 1962. Pp. 390–403.

Kuehn, A. A. "Mathematical Models of Consumer Behavior." In J. W. Newman, Ed., *On Knowing the Consumer.* New York: Wiley, 1966. Pp. 193–200.

Kuehn, A. A. and Day, R. L. "Strategy of Product Quality." *Harvard Business Review,* **10,** 100–110 (1962).

Kuehn, A. A. and Day, R. L. "Probabilistic Models of Consumer Buying Behavior." *Journal of Marketing,* **28,** 27–31 (1964).

Kuehn, A. A. and Rohloff, A. C. "New Dimensions in Analysis of Brand Switching." In Webster, Ed., *New Directions in Marketing,* American Marketing Association Proceedings, 1965, pp. 297–308.

Lawrence, R. J. "Consumer Brand Choice—A Random Walk?" *Journal of Marketing Research,* **12,** 314–324 (1975).

Lawrence, R. J. "Models of Consumer Purchasing Behavior." *Applied Statistics,* **15,** 216–233 (1966).

Lawrence, R. J. "Patterns of Buyer Behavior: Time for a New Approach?" *Journal of Marketing Research,* **6,** 137–144 (1969).

Lawrence, R. J. "Patterns of Buyer Behavior: A Rejoinder." *Journal of Marketing Research,* **7,** 120–121 (1970).

Lehmann, D. R. "Judged Similarity and Brand-switching Data as Similarity Measures." *Journal of Marketing Research,* **9,** 331–334 (1972).

Lessig, V. P. "Relating Multivariate Measures of Store Loyalty and Store Image." *Proceedings,* American Marketing Association, 1972. Pp. 305–309.

Lessig, V. P. "A Reply to Murphy and Coney." *Journal of Marketing,* **39,** 66–68 (1975).

Lessig, V. P. "Consumer Store Images and Store Loyalties." *Journal of Marketing,* **37,** 72–74 (1973).

Lipstein, B. "Tests for Test Marketing." *Harvard Business Review,* **39,** 74–77 (1961).

Lipstein, B. "A Mathematical Model of Consumer Behavior." Report to the Ninth Meeting of the ARF Operations Research Discussion Group, November 7, 1963, New York, Pp. 41–59.

Lipstein, B. "A Mathematical Model of Consumer Behavior." *Journal of Marketing Research,* **2,** 259–265 (1965).

Lipstein, B. "Test Marketing: A Perturbation in the Market Place." *Management Science,* **14,** B437–B448 (1968).

Logan, G. L. "Experimental Methods for Analyzing Consumer Buying Behavior." Unpublished master's thesis, Purdue University, 1967.

Look. "Brand Loyalty Grows Among Car Buyers." *Advertising Age,* **36,** 58 (1965).

LoSciuto, L. A., Strassman, L. H., and Wells, W. D. "Advertising Weight and the Reward Value of the Brand." *Journal of Advertising Research,* **7,** 34–38 (1967).

Maffei, R. B. "Brand Preferences and Simple Markov Process." *Operations Research,* **8,** 210–218 (1960).

Maffei, R. B. "Brand Preferences and Simple Markov Processes." In Bass, Ed., *Mathematical Models and Methods in Marketing.* Homewood, Illinois: Irwin, 1961. Pp. 109–120.

Maffei, R. B. and Lipstein, B. "Brand Switching." Report to the fourth meeting of the Operations Research Discussion Group, ARF, July 19, 1960, New York.

Mahens, J. C. "Effect of Brand Preference Upon Consumers' Perceived Taste of Turkey Meat." *Journal of Applied Psychology,* **49,** 261–263 (1964).

"Male vs. Female Influence in Buying and Brand Selection." *Journal of Marketing,* **15,** 407 (1951).

"Mamma's Shopping List Specifies Many Brands Preferred by Kids." *Journal of Marketing,* **14,** 610 (1950).

Martineau, P. "It's Time to Research the Consumer." *Harvard Business Review,* **33,** 45–54 (1955).

Mason, R. "Trend Ads Spur Brand Preference—and Research Proves It." *Journal of Marketing,* **28,** 4 (1964).

Massy, W. F. "Brand and Store Loyalty as Bases for Market Segmentation." In J. W. Newman, Ed., *On Knowing the Consumer.* New York: Wiley, 1966a. Pp. 169–172.

Massy, W. F. "Order and Homogeneity of Family Specific Brand Switching Processes." *Journal of Marketing Research,* **3,** 48–54 (1966b).

Massy, W. F., Montgomery, D. B., and Morrison, D. G., Eds., *Stochastic Models of Buying Behavior.* Boston: MIT Press, 1970.

Massy, W. F. and Morrison, D. G. "Comments on Ehrenberg's Appraisal of Brand Switching Models." *Journal of Marketing Research,* **5,** 304–308 (1968).

May, F. "Adaptive Behavior in Automobile Brand Choices." *Journal of Marketing Research,* **6,** 62–65 (1969).

May, R. E. "Effect of Social Class on Brand Loyalty." *California Management Review,* **14,** 81–87 (1971).

McConnell, J. D. "Repeat Purchase Estimation and the Linear Learning Model." *Journal of Marketing Research,* **5,** 304–308 (1968).

Mittelstaedt, R. "An Experimental Study of Consumer Brand Loyalty." *Dissertation Abstracts,* **28,** 35 (1967).

Mittelstaedt, R. "A Dissonance Approach to Repeat Purchasing Behavior." *Journal of Marketing Research,* **6,** 444–446 (1969).

Montgomery, D. B. "A Stochastic Response Model with Application to Brand Choice." *Management Science,* **15,** 323–337 (1969).

Montgomery, D. B. and Ryans, A. B. "Stochastic Models of Consumer Choice Behavior." In Ward and Robertson, Eds., *Consumer Behavior: Theoretical Sources.* Englewood Cliffs, New Jersey: Prentice-Hall, 1973. Pp. 521–576.

Morrison, D. G. "New Models of Consumer Loyalty Behavior: Aids to Setting and Evaluating Marketing Plans." In Bennett, Ed., *Marketing and Economic Development.* Chicago: AMA, 1965. Pp. 323–337.

Morrison, D. G. "Interpurchase Time and Brand Loyalty." *Journal of Marketing Research,* **3,** 289–291 (1966).

Morrison, D. G. "Testing Brand-switching Models." *Journal of Marketing Research*, **3**, 401–409 (1966).

Moulson, J. T. "Danger Signals: How to Spot Erosion in Brand Loyalty." *Printers Ink,* March 12, 1965, Pp. 55–61.

Munn, H. L. "Brand Perception as Related to Age, Income, and Education." *Journal of Marketing*, **24**, 29–34 (1960).

Murphy, J. H. and Coney, K. A. "Comments on Consumer Store Images and Store Loyalties." *Journal of Marketing*, **39**, 64–66 (1975).

Myers, J. G. "Determinants of Private Brand Attitudes." *Journal of Marketing Research*, **4**, 73–81 (1967).

"National Brands Decline." *Monetary Times*, **134**, 30–33 (May 1966).

Nordstrom, Richard D. "Analysis of Store and Brand Loyalty Behavior: An Ex Post Facto Experiment Involving New Car Purchases." Unpublished doctoral dissertation, University of Arkansas, 1974.

Olson, J. C. "Reliability and Factor Structure of Twelve Brand Loyalty Measures." Unpublished master's thesis, Purdue University, 1970.

Orr, E. W. "The Determination of Advertising Budgets for Brands." *Journal of Advertising Research*, 1963, Pp. 7–11.

Ostlund, L. E. "Evoked Set Size: Some Empirical Results." *Proceedings,* American Marketing Association, 1973. Pp. 226–230.

Padberg, D. I., Walker, F. E. and Kepner, K. W. "Measuring Consumer Brand Preference." *Journal of Farm Economics,* **49**, 723–730 (1967).

Parfitt, J. H. and Collins, B. J. K. "The Use of Consumer Panels for Brand-share Prediction." *Journal of Marketing Research*, **5**, 131–195 (1968).

Pay, W. H. "Tucson Consumer Brand Preference Study of Selected Products." *Journal of Marketing*, **28**, 89 (1964).

Perlstein, G. "A Study of the Economic Characteristics of Loyal and Disloyal Buyers." B.S. thesis, School of Industrial Management, MIT, August, 1954.

Plummer, J. T. "Life Style and Advertising: Case Studies." *Proceedings,* American Marketing Association, 1971. Pp. 290–295.

Printer's Ink. "Brand Loyalty Probed by Chicago Tribune," February 20, 1959, p. 13.

Progressive Grocer. "Consumer Dynamics in the Supermarket." Series beginning **45**, 119 (October 1965).

Ramond, C. K., Rachal, L. H., and Marks, M. R. "Brand Discrimination Among Cigarette Smokers." *Journal of Applied Psychology*, **34**, 282–284 (1950).

Rao, T. R. "Consumer Purchase Decision Processes: Stochastic Models." *Journal of Marketing Research,* **6**, 321–329 (1969).

Rao, T. R. "Time Between Purchases and Consumer Brand Choice." *Decision Sciences,* **3**, 47–55 (1972).

Rao, T. R. "Is Brand Loyalty a Criterion for Market Segmentation: Discriminant Analysis." *Decision Sciences,* **4**, 395–404 (1973).

Rohloff, A. C. "New Ways to Analyze Brand-to-Brand Competition." In Greyser, Ed., *Toward Scientific Marketing.* Chicago: AMA, 1963, Pp. 224–232.

Rollins Broadcasting. "Ads Aimed at Negro Market Build Brand Acceptance." *Advertising Age,* **34**, 57 (February 18, 1963).

Rothbert, R. "Consumer-Retailer Loyalty." *Journal of Retailing,* **47**, 72–82 (1971).

Rothman, L. J. "Research Ranges, Assortments, and Multi-brand Manufacturers." *Commentary,* **9**, 1–12 (1967).

Ruch, D. "Limitations of Current Approaches to Understanding Brand Buying Behavior." In J. W. Newman, Ed., *On Knowing the Consumer.* New York: Wiley, 1966. Pp. 173–186.

Samli, A. C. "Use of Segmentation Index to Measure Store Loyalty." *Journal of Retailing,* **51**, 51–60 (1975).

Schiffman, L. G. and Neiverth, C. J. "Measuring the Impact of Promotional Offers: An Analytic Approach." *Proceedings,* American Marketing Association, 1973. Pp. 256–260.

Scholastic Magazines, Inc. "Pop's Car Pick Is (Mostly) What Junior Would Have Chosen." *Advertising Age,* **33**, 86 (September 17, 1962).

Schutte, T. F. "The Semantics of Branding." *Journal of Marketing,* **33**, 5–12 (1969).

Sethi, S. P. "An Investigation into the Mediating Effect of Sociopsychological Variables Between Advertising Stimulus and Brand Loyalty." *Dissertation Abstracts,* **29**, 2227–2228 (1968).

Sethi, S. P. "A Comparison Between the Effect of Pulse Versus Continuous Television Advertising on Buyer Behavior." *Proceedings,* American Marketing Association, 1971. Pp. 563–567.

Sharir, Shmuel. "Brand Loyalty and the Household's Cost of Time." *The Journal of Business,* **47,** 53–55 (1974).

Sheth, J. N. "A Behavioral and Quantitative Investigation of Brand Loyalty." *Dissertation Abstracts,* **28,** 7–8 (1967).

Sheth, J. N. "How Adults Learn Brand Preference." *Journal of Advertising Research,* **8,** 25–36 (1968).

Sheth, J. N. and Venkatesan, M. "Risk-reduction Processes in Repetitive Consumer Behavior." *Journal of Marketing Research,* **5,** 307–310 (1968).

Shoemaker, R. W. and Shoaf, F. R. "Repeat Rates of Deal Purchases." *Journal of Advertising Research,* **17,** 47–53 (1977).

Shuchman, A. "Are There Laws of Consumer Behavior?" In J. Ardut, Ed., *Insights into Consumer Behavior.* Boston: Allyn & Bacon, 1968.

"Small Town Is Stronghold of Brand Loyalty, *Grit* Says." *Advertising Age,* **30,** 95 (December 14, 1959).

Smith, H. M. "Consumers Shopping Patterns in Retail Food Stores— Exploratory Study." *Journal of Marketing,* **25,** 88 (1961).

Smith, M. E. "A Laboratory Study of Consumers' Brand Preferences for Brands of Low Cost Consumer Goods." *Journal of Marketing,* **31,** 92 (1967).

Soughan, J. J. "Sales Promotion Is Only Way to Keep Fickle Customer in Camp." *Advertising Age,* **33,** 4 (1962).

Stafford, J. E. "Effects of Group Influences on Consumer Brand Preferences." *Journal of Marketing Research,* **3,** 68–74 (1966).

Stahl, G. "Create 'Pedigree' for Brand to Rebuild Users' Loyalty." *Advertising Age,* **33,** 56 (1962).

Starch, D. "Do Ad Readers Buy the Product?" *Harvard Business Review,* **36,** 49–58 (1958).

Stem, D. E. "Consumer Perception and Evaluation of Pre-purchase Risk Reduction Methods." *Dissertation Abstracts,* **37,** 1186A (1976).

Stock, J. S. "Paired Market Choice Model—A Simplified Approach to Markov Chains." In Gomez, Ed., *Innovation: Key to Marketing Progress.* Chicago: AMA, 1963. Pp. 99–105.

Suppes, P. C. and Atkinson, R. C. *Markov Processes.* Stanford, California: Stanford University Press, 1960.

Styan, G. and Smith, H. "Markov Chains Applied to Marketing." *Journal of Marketing Research,* **1,** 50–55 (1964).

Tankersley, C. B. "An Attitudinal Approach to the Investigation of Brand Loyalty." Unpublished doctoral dissertation, University of Cincinnati, 1974.

Tarpey, L. X. "Behaviorism and Store Loyalty: A Theoretical Analysis." *Working Paper in Business Administration, No. BA8.* University of Kentucky, 1977.

Tate, R. S. "The Supermarket Battle for Store Loyalty." *Journal of Marketing,* **25,** 8–13 (1961).

Telser, L. G. "The Demand for Branded Goods as Estimated from Consumer Panel Data." *Review of Economics and Statistics,* **44,** 300–324 (1962).

Twedt, D. W. "How Important to Marketing Strategy is the 'heavy-user.' " *Journal of Marketing,* **28,** 71–72 (1964).

Twedt, D. W. "How Does Brand Awareness-Attitude Effect Marketing Strategy?" *Journal of Marketing,* **31,** 64–66 (1967).

Tyler, W. D. "The Image, the Brand, and the Consumer." *Journal of Marketing,* **22,** 162–165 (1957).

Uhl, K. P. "Shareowner Brand Preferences." *Journal of Business,* **35,** 57–69 (1962).

Uhl, K. P. and Schoner, B. *Marketing Research: Information Systems and Decision Making.* New York: Wiley, 1969.

Waung, S. "A Multivariate Analysis of Physician Prescribing Behavior." *Dissertation Abstracts,* **36,** 408A (1975).

Weber, J. E. and Hansen, R. M. "The Majority Effect and Brand Choice." *Journal of Marketing Research,* **9,** 320–323 (1972).

Webster, F. E. "The 'Deal-prone' Consumer." *Journal of Marketing Research,* **2,** 186–189 (1965).

Wells, W. D. "Measuring Readiness to Buy." *Harvard Business Review,* **39,** 81–87 (1961).

Wells, W. D. and Beard, A. D. "Personality and Consumer Behavior." In S. Ward and T. S. Robertson, Eds., *Consumer Behavior: Theoretical Sources.* Englewood Cliffs, New Jersey: Prentice-Hall, 1973. Pp. 141–199.

Werbel, R. A. "A Multivariate Analysis of Brand Loyalty for Purchasers of New Cars and Major Household Appliances." *Dissertation Abstracts,* **33,** 5906-A (1973).

Wheeler, David R. "Brand Loyalties: Qualitative, Quantitative, or Both?" *Journal of the Academy of Marketing Science,* **2,** 651 (1974).

Wiggelsworth, F. G. "Marketing Branded Goods in Malaya." *Journal of Marketing,* **19,** 84, (1954).

Wind, Y. "Industrial Buying Behavior: Source Loyalty in the Purchase of Industrial Components." Unpublished doctoral dissertation, Stanford University, 1966.

Wind, Y. "Brand Loyalty and Vulnerability." In A. G. Woodside, J. N. Sheth, and P. D. Bennett, Eds., *Consumer and Industrial Buying Behavior.* New York: North-Holland, 1977. Pp. 313–319.

Wind, Y. and Frank, R. E. "Interproduct Household Loyalty to Brands." *Journal of Marketing Research,* **6,** 434–435 (1969).

Winick, C. "Relationships Among Personality Needs, Objective Factors, and Brand Choice: A Re-examination." *Journal of Business,* **34,** 61–66 (1961).

Winn, P. R. "The Determinants of Consumer Deal Proneness: A Multivariate Analysis." Unpublished doctoral dissertation, University of Illinois, 1971.

Woodlock, J. "Fourth Purchase of Product is Most Significant." *Advertising Age,* **34,** 64 (1963).

Yankelovich, D. "New Criteria for Market Segmentation." *Harvard Business Review,* **42,** 83–90 (1964).

Zipf, G. K. "Brand Names and Related Social Phenomena." *American Journal of Psychology,* **63,** 342–366 (1950).

Zipf, G. K. "A Note on Brand-names and Related Economic Phenomena." *Econometrica,* **18,** 260–263 (1950).

Author Index

Ajzen, I., 6, 109, 110
Anderson, B. B., 3, 116
Anderson, E. E., 21, 29, 30, 40, 42, 117
Aronson, E., 56
Axelrod, J. L., 64

Barbour, F., 106
Bass, F. M., 3, 4, 8
Becker, G. S., 69
Bellenger, D. N., 27, 29, 55
Bennett, P. D., 20, 29, 49
Berning, C. A. K., 118
Bettman, J. R., 106, 114
Bodi, M. J., 46, 60
Bohrnstedt, G. W., 75
Bourne, L. E., 76, 77
Bradley, R. A., 50
Braunstein, M. L., 113
Brown, G. H., 10, 11, 12, 13, 15, 17, 24, 29, 35, 36, 40, 83
Bruner, J. S., 77
Bubb, P. L., 24, 25, 29, 40
Burford, R. L., 24, 29, 38, 63
Busato-Schach, J., 114
Byrne, D., 109, 110

Campbell, D. T., 52, 92, 98
Campbell, J. R., 72, 93, 97, 98
Carlsmith, J. M., 56
Carman, J. M., 3, 23, 29, 39, 116

Carnap, R., 79
Chaplin, J. P., 75
Charlton, P., 26, 29, 35
Chestnut, R. W., 22, 27, 50, 92, 106, 107, 111, 113, 114, 115, 118
Churchill, H., 11, 12, 13, 29, 35
Clokey, J. D., 8
Collins, B. E., 6
Cook, T. D., 72, 97
Copeland, M. T., 10, 11, 19, 29, 35, 52, 112
Cronbach, L. J., 93, 98
Cunningham, R. M., 12, 13, 15, 17, 19, 23, 25, 26, 29, 35, 36, 39, 45, 46, 53, 56, 61, 83

Darden, W. R., 6, 21, 49, 62
Day, G. S., 16, 19, 27, 29, 45, 53, 56, 60, 62, 63, 112, 116
Dietvorst, T. F., 118
Dommermuth, W. P., 17, 29, 38
Douglas, S. P., 3
Dupuy, G. M., 26, 29, 40

Ehrenberg, A. S. C., 3, 14, 16, 26, 29, 35, 83, 86
Engel, J. E., 80, 89, 116
Enis, B. M., 24, 38, 63

Farley, J., 16, 29, 39, 44
Fishbein, M., 6, 48, 109, 110

Fisher, W., 114, 118
Fiske, D. W., 52, 92, 98
Fogg, C. D., 2
Frank, R. E., 3, 15, 16, 18, 29, 36,
    37, 38, 45, 46, 60, 63, 83
Fry, J. N., 25, 26, 29, 37

Geiselman, R. D., 116
Goodhardt, G. J., 83
Griffitt, W., 110
Gruber, A., 23
Guest, L. P., 10, 11, 16, 19, 25, 29,
    47, 48
Guilford, J. P., 74
Guiltinan, J. P., 22, 29, 48

Hall, C. S., 87
Harary, F., 15
Hartigan, J. A., 79
Heeler, R. M., 93
Herniter, J. D., 3
Hovland, C. I., 20
Howard, J. A., 18, 83, 106, 111
Hughes, G. D., 105

Insko, C. A., 6

Jacoby, J., 5, 6, 19, 20, 22, 27, 29,
    45, 48, 49, 50, 51, 53, 56, 57, 60,
    61, 62, 63, 69, 80, 82, 83, 89, 95,
    98, 106, 107, 111, 112, 113, 114,
    116, 117, 118
Jarvis, L. P., 6, 22, 29, 49
Jenkins, J. G., 10
Jeuland, A., 4
Jones, W., 22, 50
Juster, F. T., 22, 23, 50

Kaplan, A., 86
Kassarjian, H. H., 20, 29, 49
Kerlinger, F. N., 96
Kiesler, C. A., 6, 116
Krawiec, T. S., 75
Kuehn, A. A., 13, 14, 15, 16, 93
Kyner, D. B., 5, 53, 80, 89, 98, 112

Lamont, L. M., 116, 117
Linder, S. B., 69
Lindzey, G., 87
Link, H. C., 10
Lipstein, B., 4, 14, 15, 26, 29, 35, 37,
    46
Livesy, F., 24, 29, 41
Lodahl, T. M., 18, 36, 37, 38, 45, 46,
    60, 63, 83
Luce, M. E., 50
Lutz, R. J., 27, 29, 53, 57, 62

McCann, J. M., 25, 29, 36
McConnell, J. D., 17, 29, 36, 53, 117
McGregor, D., 11
McGuire, W. J., 107, 119
McHale, H. P., 116
Martin, W. S., 6, 21, 27, 29, 34, 49,
    54, 62
Massaro, D. W., 72, 106, 107
Massy, W. F., 18, 29, 36, 38, 45, 46,
    60, 63, 83, 104
Meehl, P. E., 98
Miller, N., 6
Mitchell, A. A., 63
Monroe, K. B., 22, 29, 48
Muderrisoglu, A., 106

Nebergall, R., 20
Newman, J. W., 26, 27, 29, 54, 116
Nicosia, F. M., 106
Nordstrom, R. D., 26, 29, 41
Nunnally, J. C., 74, 77, 86, 91, 92,
    93, 95, 96, 97

Olson, J. C., 5, 19, 29, 45, 48, 49, 51,
    56, 57, 60, 61, 62, 63, 69, 80, 95,
    106, 116, 117

Park, W. C., 80, 89, 112
Paul, G. W., 24, 38, 63
Payne, J. W., 106
Pessemier, E. A., 13, 17, 29, 53, 57,
    84
Plutchik, R., 72, 73, 74, 77, 78

Polli, R., 3
Posner, , M. I., 113

Ray, M. L., 93
Reynolds, F. D., 6, 8, 21, 29, 49, 62
Rothe, J. T., 116, 117
Rice, W., 63

Selltiz, C., 71, 72, 74, 77, 78, 94
Shapiro, B. P., 117
Sherif, C., 20
Sherif, M., 20
Sheth, J. N., 18, 29, 38, 46, 50, 80,
    83, 89, 106, 111, 112
Speller, D. E., 21
Stanton, W. W., 27, 55
Steinberg, E., 27, 55
Swan, J. E., 26, 29, 41
Szybillo, G. J., 51, 52, 61, 62, 63,

114, 116 117

Tarpey, L. X., 80
Terry, M. E., 50
Torgerson, W. S., 9
Towle, J. G., 27, 29, 34, 54
Tucker, W. T., 17, 29, 36, 53

van Rest, D. J., 24, 25, 29, 40

Weigl, K. C., 114, 118
Wells, W. D., 8
Werbel, R. A., 26, 27, 29, 54, 116
Wilcox, J. B., 6, 22, 29, 49
Wind, Y., 24, 112
Winn, P. R., 27, 29, 53, 57, 62
Winters, F. W., 92
Woodside, A. G., 8
Wright, P., 4, 92, 106

Subject Index

Advertising, 11, 116
Affect, states of, 107-112, 114, 115
Assimilation-Contrast, 20
Attitudes, brand loyal, 6, 19, 20, 51, 112

Bayesian multivariate analysis, 27
Beliefs, 107-112, 114, 115
Behavior, brand loyal, 9, 19, 45, 112
Brand allegiance, 40
Brand insistence, 10, 52, 62
Brand preference, 47, 61
Brand runs;
    average length of, 37, 45, 60, 91, 91
    number of, 36, 46, 60
Brand switching, 5, 15

Chicago Tribune, 10
Cognitive activities, *see* Information
    processing
Commitment, brand, 17
    psychological, 9, 84, 89, 104
    stated brand, 26, 52, 53, 55, 62
Concept, 72-79, 85, 86, 89, 90, 92,
    94, 95, 97-99
Construct, 77, 92, 94, 95, 97, 104

Decision-making unit, 81, 83
Definition;
    conceptual, 41, 68, 70, 71, 74, 80,
    85, 86, 89, 90, 96, 99

operational, 7, 68, 70, 71, 73, 74,
    80, 94, 96, 99
Determinism, 4, 30
Disloyalty, 47, 65, 83, 98

Emotional response, *see* Affect, states
    of
Entropy, measure of, 23, 39, 61
Estimate by elimination, 40, 61
Evoked set, 83, 111

Factor analytic models, *see* Factor
    scores
Factor scores, 38, 46, 50, 60
Forecasting, 8
FRA, 25, 36, 60

Habit, 16
Hard-core, 15, 26, 35, 60
Heuristic;
    brand name, 114, 115
    decision, 112, 113

Inertia, *see* Entropy, measure of;
    Estimate by elimination
Information processing, 105-107, 112,
    115, 118
Information search, 26, 54, 62, 111,
    114
Information storage, *see* Memory,
    long-term

Intention, behavioral, 107, 108, 110-112, 114, 115
Intent-to-purchase, 50, 62

Likert scaling, *see* Scaling, psychographic
Loyalty;
  bank, 25, 26, 37, 60
  Bayesian, 53, 62
  brand name, 48, 61
  cognitive, 22, 49, 62
  composite store, 55, 62
  consumer, 21
  dealer/agency, 26, 41, 61
  divided, 12, 36, 60
  dual-brand, 12, 25, 36, 60
  general-brand, 63
  intentional, 19
  multibrand, 43, 47, 49, 51, 63, 83
  multidimensional, 18
  new-resident, 40, 61
  private-brand, 24, 40, 61
  rental brand, 41, 61
  source, 24
  spurious, 19, 56
  store, 24, 27, 49, 56, 65
  triple-brand, 25, 36, 60
  unstable, 12, 36, 60
Loyalty index, 19, 38, 53, 61

Market share, 2, 30, 101, 102, 104
Market-share concept , 12, 13, 35, 45, 60
Markov chains, 4
Markov process, 14
Measurement, unit of, 42, 65
Measurement level;
  macro, 8, 21, 29, 30
  micro, 8, 21, 29, 30
Measurement type;
  attitude, 9, 29
  behavioral, 9, 29
  composite, 9, 29
Measures;
  behavioroid, 56

composite, 26, 52, 56
Memory, long-term, 107, 108, 113
Methodology, process, 27
Model;
  linear-learning, 14
  probabilistic, 4

N_{ar}, 16, 39, 44, 61
N_m, 16, 39, 61
Nondurables, 1, 107

Ordered alternative sorting, 51

Package search, 54, 62
Panels, consumer, 11
Preference, constancy of, 48, 51, 61
Price-until-switching, 13, 53, 56, 62
Probability;
  repeat purchase, 15, 37, 60
  return purchase, 15, 37, 60
Probability of repurchase, 15, 37, 60
Product importance, 52
Purchase;
  exclusive, 35, 60
  percent of, 44, 91, 92
  probability of, 35, 44, 50
  proportion of, 15, 26, 35
  see also Market-Share concept
Purchase probability scale, 22, 23

Ratio;
  lost-gained, 13, 39, 61
  R/A, 20, 22, 48
Region;
  acceptance, 48, 50, 51, 61
  modified measure of, 49, 62
  neutrality, 48, 51, 61
  number of brands:
    in acceptance, 49, 61
    in rejection, 49, 62
  range of, 48, 61
Reliability, 45, 47, 58, 59, 65
  test-retest, 46, 51, 52, 56, 57, 63
Rental agreements, 25. *See also* Loyalty, rental brand

Risk, perceived, 52
Rule, decision, *see* Heuristic, brand
    name

S_{ar}, 16, 39, 61
Scaling, psychographic, 49, 62
Segmentation, 102-105
Sensitivity, 45-47, 51, 52, 57-59, 64,
    65
Shopping matrix, 38, 60
S_m, 16, 39, 61
Stages;
    analysis of, 106
    functions of, 107, 112
    processing of, 106
    structures of, 107, 110, 112
Staying time, average, 15, 37, 60
Stochastic models, 4, 15-17
Stochastic process, 4, 14
Stochastic theories, 2
Switching, *see* Brand switching

Theory, 8, 85, 86, 89
Theory;
    communicative function, 88, 89
    descriptive function, 86, 89
    explanative function, 88, 89
    heuristic function, 88, 89
    organizational function, 87
    predivtive function, 88, 89
Three-in-a-row criterion, 36, 44, 45,
    60
Two-thirds criterion, 35, 60

Validity, 45, 47, 51, 58, 59, 65, 90
    concurrent, 93
    construct, 47, 57, 86, 90, 96-99
    content, 93
    convergent, 27, 52, 94, 95
    criterion-related, 93
    discriminant, 27, 52
    face, 92
    predictive, 46, 93